D1571290

Dramatic Allegory

Dramatic Allegory

Lindsay's
Ane Satyre of the Thrie Estaitis

Joanne Spencer Kantrowitz

UNIVERSITY OF NEBRASKA PRESS · LINCOLN

Chapter 1 originally appeared in slightly different form in *Studies in Scottish Literature* 10 (July 1972): 18–32, and is reprinted with the permission of the Editor. Chapter 6 originally appeared in different form in *Comparative Drama* 7 (Spring 1973): 68–82, and is reprinted by permission of the Editors.

Publishers on the Plains

UNP

The publication of this book was assisted by a grant from
The Andrew W. Mellon Foundation.

Library of Congress Cataloging in Publication Data

Kantrowitz, Joanne Spencer, 1931–
   Dramatic allegory.

   Includes bibliographical references and index.
   1. Lindsay, Sir David, fl. 1490–1555. Ane satyre of the thrie estaitis. I. Title.
PR2659.L5A734 1975 822'.2 74–76134
ISBN 0–8032–0842–1

For my grandmother
Mary Fleming Fraser
(1872–1959)
She made all the difference

CONTENTS

Dramatic Allegory

Introduction

Whatever critics have thought of it, allegory is rarely described as "dramatic." Yet I use the term deliberately to mean drama cast in the form of allegory enacted onstage, and to emphasize that connection between the allegory which is narrative and the drama which is called conventionally, if clumsily, the morality or the moral play. Like so many others, this book began as an attempt to comprehend that puzzling group of plays produced in England during the fifteenth and sixteenth centuries. This is a drama that scarcely exists outside the groves of Academe; few of us in America have even seen these plays performed. The *Thrie Estaitis* was successfully revived at the Edinburgh Festival in 1948 and has enjoyed a vigorous stage life in Britain ever since. The general audience knows that play, at least, in Britain, but few Americans have ever heard of it nor of other plays like it.

Strangely, modern drama in the West has taken a turn recently which brings it closer to the pre-Shakespearean tradition. Drama, it seems, has a life of its own apart from formal literary criticism. In 1966, I attended the British production in New York of Peter Weiss's *Marat/Sade*. The play was performed on a proscenium stage in a conventional theater although it seemed made for the open stage of the newer dramaturgy. That winter, the play was fashionable in New York, but the audience came prepared for titillation and went away in confusion. I have never seen an American theater audience so silent during an intermission, and silence in New York suggests that people have lost their customary confidence and are waiting to see what the "proper" response is. I have seen similar responses to Pinter plays, and a taste for Beckett or Ionesco is, of course, a literary-intellectual status symbol. Although the new theater has been with us since the early 1950s, we are still living in a time when the conventions of drama are in transit between the late nineteenth-century masters and those who have yet to appear. We still talk of drama as conflict, of heroes or protagonists, of scenes and acts, but we talk more of what a specific play is about, we read more about theater as ritual, about the audience as part of the play. That is, we seem to be in a period when drama—and literature—is more concerned with meaning and with moving toward and into the audience. The accompanying interest in allegory among critics of modern literature seems to result from that modern search for meaning. Suddenly, a topic that was scarcely fashionable ten years ago has taken on new life. We are met with allegories on every hand, so that simple plain statement seems lost and every art one meets must have underlying significance. (This can lead to literary indigestion in a perfectly reasonable reaction against interpretation.)

But these modern confusions are not the problems of the literary historian, however much they may tickle the edges of his existence as a part of the audience for modern art. Professionally, one sees the parallels between the old and the new, but the old is so unexplored that the process of revitalization has scarcely begun. Popularization and the creation of parallels can hardly occur before the scholar has done his work. Some might wish this book were more ambitious; a few have uged me to extend it farther than it goes, but I have declined to do so. Perhaps it is perverse of me. One wants, after all, to make the large statement and to shake the battlements a bit, but I have a prejudice against big books right now. The morality play has too frequently been the object of sweeping generalizations while the work of detailed analysis and explication has scarcely begun.[1] What we need now is the spadework for that definitive study of the pre-Shakespearean drama which someone will write in the future. Perhaps, then, we will be able to see more clearly the connections between the old drama and the new and to think more cogently on the social reasons why didactic literature should languish and then revive.

As it stands now, the standard literary histories of the morality play often read like a series of plot summaries. Since such bare descriptions are so much alike, the plays soon threaten to become indistinguishable. Yet, one realizes, the relative paucity of research on specific texts makes the task of the generalizer impossible, for without a body of specific studies, the historian must depend on his own reading of a widely varied set of plays, few of them thoroughly explored. Many are not even available in authoritative editions.

Indeed, we are not even agreed on terminology. The drama from ca. 1400 to ca. 1570 still suffers the classifications developed during the late nineteenth century. We are given "moralities, mysteries, and miracles." The latter two terms account for what are now called "the cycle plays" and those shorter texts, like the Digby *Mary Magdalene*, which share the topics of biblical drama. These are dated in the fifteenth century, although the cycles continued to be performed well into the sixteenth century, just as Chekov and Ibsen continue to be performed in our own time. *Moral play* seems to be a general category for everything that is not biblical in its subject matter (although there are exceptions like *Godly Queen Hester* or Heywood's "comedies"). *Mystery* and *miracle*, then, describe the content of particular plays, while *morality* seems to describe a play which has a didactic purpose. Yet all three describe a corpus of drama which was written before the new, Aristotelian poetics were current in England and before the decided shift toward an essentially mimetic drama with its focus on characterization. One day, perhaps, we shall have an account which unifies this sprawling and inexact period between the first survivors of plays in English and the emergence of the Elizabethan theater. Until then, we must shape the pieces as we find them—or rest content with still another effort which derives from Tucker Brooke and the scholars of 1910, seasoned with the emphases of the intervening years, but still proceding on the basis of the same definitions. Despite some few signs of shifts in scholarly thinking, the plays are still described primarily in terms of story, in terms of psychomachia, or classifed in terms which were developed for the later drama.[2]

This situation has begun to change slightly within the last few years, spurred largely by some remarkable work on the history of staging by Glynne Wickham, Richard Southern, and T. W. Craik.[3] Yet work on the questions of dramatic form has progressed less rapidly, with most of the effort concentrated on the cycle plays. The bibliography of work on individual plays—except for the cycles—is surprisingly small, while most of the books which deal with the morality play are necessarily cursory because their sweep is too wide or because they examine that drama as a means toward understanding Elizabethan theater. The latter element (the more common one) usually limits observation to those characteristics which seem most like the later plays.[4]

Although the sirens of greater theorizing beckon, I have chosen a humbler course here, because I think the material will not sustain such theory until the evidence exists in much greater detail. Instead, I have closely examined one major play and have chosen to do a narrow, specialized study in the hope that such precision will suggest a new way for describing that allegorical drama which uses fiction as a tool for reasoning, with plot and character as counters in a developing argument enacted for an audience. What is offered here, then, is a discussion of Sir David Lindsay's *Ane Satyre of the Thrie Estaitis*, selected for study because it is complex enough to pose serious problems of interpretation and to provide substantial comparison and contrast with a fairly wide set of literary materials. This approach reverses one way of studying drama: some study many plays of a period to understand its greatest dramatists; I have studied Lindsay's play to understand the drama of which it is a part. I have also tried to set the *Thrie Estaitis* within the context of its artistic tradition, seeing that as the vernacular materials of the late Middle Ages. This analysis of the *Thrie Estaitis* results in what I trust is a new approach to the morality play and in a series of proposals for further specific study.

Because the play is Scottish, some readers might insist on more specific emphasis on Scottish materials than they will find here. Although I have read widely in Scottish literature, I found few direct and clear parallels to the materials in Lindsay's play. Since I view Scottish literature as part of British literature, I saw no reason to restrict the materials used for purposes of analysis: linguistic boundaries are not as rigid as political boundaries when it comes to the reading and writing of books. As a result, I use materials from both the English and Scottish traditions, hoping that the comparisons will speak for their own validity. Similarly, I have not written a specific study of Lindsay's works. While such an effort would be well worth doing, I have been interested in Lindsay's poems only as they provide context for his play. The play itself is the only drama which has survived for sixteenth-century Scotland; it has no peers if we exclude the morality plays written south of the border but within the same tradition. And it is the tradition of the allegorical drama which provides the central focus of this study.

In its earliest stages, this work began with the books of E. N. S. Thompson, W. R. MacKenzie, Willard Farnham, and C. S. Lewis.

Most current studies of the morality play do, for they are governed by assumptions developed by these authorities; I hope that my reasons for divergence will become self-evident as this book unfolds. Unlike the work of MacKenzie and Farnham, this book does not search for incipient signs of the drama's developing powers of characterization or of radical shifts in thought. Having abandoned the theories of Creizenach, Thompson, and Lewis, it also denies the "psychomachia principle." This approach hampers the discussion of both narrative and dramatic allegory with a view which essentially reduces those art forms to an origin in Prudentius's poem, written more than a thousand years before the poems and plays here discussed. Learning from all these scholars, yet following none, I have attempted to form a different set of descriptive criteria for the morality play.

These criteria are based on a view of allegory as an expository art which works through fictions turned to many differing purposes. Obviously, such a description operates outside the terms usually used in the discussion of allegory. It does not describe allegory as extended metaphor or personification. Nor does it employ the terms of the fourfold method with its figural interpretation. This is a view of allegory which concentrates on the relation between fable (or fiction) and theme (or argument). While I began with those allegories Lewis calls "moral" or "homiletic," that term, too, rapidly became clumsy, for this study emphasizes the differences between allegories which Lewis essentially placed in a residual category as nonerotic, that is, not concerned with "the allegory of love." Yet, while they do indeed "moralize," that is, express a point of view about some facet of life, they utilize a variety of fictions and express a variety of viewpoints employed toward that "moral" end. Like the term *morality play, moral allegory* implies similarities which are not supported by the individual works themselves. The problem of comparison and contrast lies at the center of both narrative and dramatic allegory, for similar fictions may demonstrate quite different themes, and similar themes may be embodied in different fictions. For myself, I prefer the term *didactic*—not in its recently pejorative sense, but as a description of a work of art whose main purpose is to convey intellectual meaning instead of imitated experience (mimetic art) and whose consequent structure reflects a greater emphasis on theme than on fable. I hope these terms and distinctions will become less abstract as the argument of this book progresses, for, in the end, the critical principle is no better than the practice.

The practice, here, is a study of *Ane Satyre of the Thrie Estaitis*. This study is divided into two sorts of efforts which may be stated quite simply as *what* and *how*. Hopefully, this statement is not as simple-minded as it sounds. With the *Thrie Estaitis*, as with most moralities, the first problem is one of precisely understanding what is happening in the action of the play. We begin, then, by asking what the play is about. Once that question of content is answered, we than ask how that content is presented, a question which examines the form of the play.

In the past, Lindsay's drama has been regarded as a series of loosely connected "interludes," a perception that recognizes the essentially episodic nature of a plot which is not geared to the exposition of a protagonist's action. The first half of the play seems clear enough. A king called Rex Humanitas is seduced by a lady called Sensualitie and his kingdom corrupted by courtiers and vices until a divine emissary forces reformation. In the second half of the play, that reformation is discussed and effected, but the action occurs with little use of the characters employed in the first part of the action, and the apparent protagonist, the king, hardly acts at all. Yet, despite this lack of a clear protagonist and a clear plot line, the play possesses its own sort of unity and development which is achieved through an artistic method unfamiliar to our modern assumptions about the nature of dramatic action.

In order to isolate the implicit methods for achieving that development and unity, one must first identify the materials out of which the play is constructed; that is, one must, in a certain sense, learn how to read the play. In this area, the *Thrie Estaitis* poses three interconnected problems. The first is a problem of date, for until this issue is decided, the background of the play in the politics of its time cannot be defined precisely. And because the play is essentially political in nature, one cannot proceed very far in comprehension until that historical background is supplied. The history reconstructed here, in the second chapter, does not read the play as a dramatic *roman á clef*: the action presented on stage seems to be a generalized depiction of Scottish politics rather than a specific representation of specific events and people. Yet, general as it is, the action loses much significance if viewed apart from the events which occurred during Lindsay's lifetime. Such material, too, helps to reconstruct the probable response of a contemporary audience that shared, with the play's author, the troubled history of Scotland before the final split between reformers and Roman Catholics.

Once that basic framework of historical relevance is established, I turn toward a further question of meaning. Having examined political events, I next move to an exploration of the terms in which those events are discussed. Here, in the third chapter, relevant texts enable us to discover a series of ideas which the *Thrie Estaitis* shares with many predecessors. Basically, these ideas center on the opposition between reason and sensuality as those two qualities affect human actions, and, particularly, as they influence the state and development of human society in the government of nations. Chapter three does not exhaust the available materials on reason and sensuality. It does not, for example, search out sermons and philosophical treatises to frame its generalizations. Although such materials might be useful, they seemed somewhat superfluous when the ideas are so readily available in the less specialized and more popular texts of the period: those in the *speculum principis* tradition, both as its materials appear in handbooks for rulers and in the work of Lydgate and Elyot, and those which are utilized in narrative allegory.

With the third chapter, the attempt to describe the subject of the play ends, and we turn from the *what* to the *how*, to the problems of artistic method. (These cannot be discussed, after all, until the material of the play is well enough understood to deal with similarities and differences in the treatment of comparable subjects.) For the purposes of our analysis, then, we approach the problem of artistic method in the *Thrie Estaitis* with a separate discussion of narrative allegory in order to discover the practices which the narrative mode shares with the dramatic mode. The ten texts selected for discussion date from the end of the fourteenth century to the mid-sixteenth century and are divided into two groups. The first group of six allegories suggests the range which exists in subject matter and handling; the second group is limited to political texts in order to suggest the varieties of fiction available to the political allegorist. Here, allegory emerges as an artistic method which may be used with different kinds of materials in many different proportions and in many different ways. Making a few simple observations about the nature of allegorical action, character, time, and space, we arrive at a view of allegory which sees it as the exposition of an argument, with a thesis and its accompanying rhetoric. Such an argument is designed to persuade and delight its readers through the use of an allegorical fable which may be metaphorical or literal in its basic conception.

Given this examination of allegory, we then turn at last to the basic question of dramatic form, prepared now to ask a different set of questions, based on a view of the morality play as dramatic allegory. The *Thrie Estaitis* is set, once again, among comparable materials. This time, we select three "political" morality plays: *Magnificence, King Johan,* and *Respublica.* Here, the analysis revolves around three areas: the definition of subject and theme (the viewpoint taken within each subject); the creation of allegorical materials to represent each theme; and, finally, the effects produced by the structure of character and action. Briefly, we conclude that *Magnificence* is not, strictly, a political play at all, and that *Respublica* breaks down as allegorical statement, while the *Thrie Estaitis* and *King Johan* remain as sustained political allegories using different means, however, to achieve different degrees of satiric response. By comparison, the satiric effect of the *Thrie Estaitis* is seen as part of a continuum situated between the lighter, comic effect of *Respublica* and the vitriolic satire of *King Johan.*

With this, the experiment in analysis ends. Hopefully, this detailed study of one play has demonstrated an approach which will ease the exploration of other plays of the period and of other allegorical and didactic works. Briefly, I have attempted to isolate those areas which form the core of *Ane Satyre of the Thrie Estaitis.* Such areas, obviously, will vary from play to play. Few plays, I imagine, are so closely tied to the problems of dating and contemporary history—these are peculiar to the text at hand. Yet most must be set within the context of the relevent intellectual milieu in order to understand what the writer, in his own era, might have assumed as common knowledge in a literate audience. Once the basic questions of meaning are understood, one then turns to questions of aesthetics. Here, I have taken the structural approach, a means which I believe grasps the basic shape of the play better than the many other methods available to modern critics. Obviously, this approach omits other kinds of considerations which are also worthy of study: the questions of language, both linguistic and aesthetic; the relationship of the play to Lindsay's poems; questions of influence, both foreign and vernacular; and many other matters of that ilk.[5] This study, then, purports to be no more than an outline but, if I may be tedious for a moment, an outline which draws together materials and methods somewhat neglected in the past.

Still, in such a study, many more problems emerged which had to be left unsolved. This is particularly true in the realm of critical theory where the reconstruction of pre-Elizabethan ideas about the nature of literature is still less than satisfactory.[6] As one reads, glimmerings of other modes of thought appear, modes of thought about literature different from those which grew up in the latter half of the sixteenth century when a turn toward more literal methods of representation gradually displaced the allegorical in popularity. Nevertheless, I have declined to follow these possibilities for further exploration. It seemed both more necessary and more relevant to concentrate on a few basic topics which might produce a clarification of one ill-understood morality play, before proceeding to the larger areas. These larger issues, ultimately, can be precisely studied only after the work of basic comprehension is accomplished, at least in part. From my own point of view, it is too soon and the materials are too vaguely comprehended for the creation of sound generalizations about the nature of the morality play. Generalize we must; but we should also recognize the tentative and limited nature of such generalizations at this point.

In the last chapter, "The Morality Reconsidered," I have indulged in a few of these generalizations. There, the dominant characterization of the plays as *psychomachia* is examined in more detail by returning to an early statement of that position, a view which rests on the assumptions of earlier scholarship. Although few scholars still subscribe to those assumptions, the description which resulted from them is still tacitly accepted by most people who discuss the morality play. Besides this basic attack, which seems necessary if the field is to be cultivated, I suggest several areas which will require further exploration before any general description of an aesthetic for the morality play can be formed in terms of that central necessity, the witness of contemporary sources. Although the approach developed in this book arises from the texts themselves, some less inductive evidence appears to exist for the view that allegory is essentially argument.

In some respects, then, this book raises more questions than it settles. An imperfect state of affairs, indeed. But the alternative is worse: to become like Casaubon, the scholar in *Middlemarch*, who accumulated notes and ideas until the last dong of doom sounded, with his book still unwritten. This book must present itself as only an *essai*, a try, in that old sense of the word which comforts the human in us all. I hope that its questions are relevant and that this attempt may help others to explore the early drama, so that one day a new body of knowledge will exist for a new generation of scholars to assume, to challenge, and to change.

NOTES

1. Bibliographical notes appear in chapter 6 where the problems of the morality play are considered in more specific detail.

2. For explorations of terminology, see A. P. Rossiter, *English Drama from the Earliest Times to Elizabeth* (London: Hutchinson and Co., 1950), pp. 81, 95, 106; Glynne Wickham, *Early English Stages 1300–1660*, vol. 1 (London: Routledge and Kegan Paul, 1959–63), pp. 234–35; E. K. Chambers, *The Medieval Stage*, 2 vols. (Oxford: Clarendon Press, 1903), 2:151; Allardyce Nicoll's summary of " 'Tragical-Comical-Historical-Pastoral': Elizabeth Dramatic Nomenclature," *Bulletin of the John Rylands Library* 43 (1960): 79; and Alan C. Dessen, "The Morall as an Elizabethan Dramatic Kind: An Exploratory Essay," *Comparative Drama* 5 (1971): 138–58.

3. Wickham, *Early English Stages*, vols. 1 and 2, pt. 1. Richard Southern, *The Medieval Theatre in the Round* (London: Faber and Faber, 1957). T. W. Craik, *The Tudor Interlude* (Leicester: Leicester University Press, 1958).

4. Some scholars of Elizabethan drama are beginning to move toward newer syntheses on form. See, for example, Charles O. McDonald's *The Rhetoric of Tragedy: Form in Stuart Drama* (Amherst: University of Massachusetts Press, 1966) and Jonas A. Barish, "The New Theater and the Old," in *Reinterpretations of Elizabethan Drama*, ed. Norman Rabkin (New York: Columbia University Press, 1969), pp. 1–31. Barish discusses the modern move toward "antirealism" beginning with the interest in Brecht and Artaud. Such observations use modern critical positions, however, and do not attempt to develop theories on the basis of literary history. For a counter to the usual method, see the work of Hans-Robert Jauss who raises incisive questions about modern literary theories. He argues that such theories reflect modern literature and, as such, are only partial aesthetics which do not sit comfortably on the literature of the past.

5. This does not mean that other materials may not be relevant. Continental Reformation plays and French farce have been suggested as relevant to Lindsay's work, and they may well be. Both areas remain unexplored. I have also declined to adopt the medieval/Renaissance division of history. Such a sharp distinction of time is an impediment when one is considering the vernacular tradition from 1400 to 1555 (the approximate dates for materials discussed here). As a result, I often use the term *medieval* when referring to sixteenth century texts which use the older ideas and literary conventions. Obviously, this is a convenience in writing and implies *not* a value judgment but a view of the period which emphasizes continuity.

6. See the discussion of rhetoric and dramatic commentaries in chapter 6.

Chapter 1

Date

To begin a critical study with a dating problem is, perhaps, to demonstrate once again the futility of separating the scholarly and the critical functions. Before discussing artistic method, one must establish an interpretation; before interpretation is possible, one must have a clear idea of the time and place within which the text exists. This is particularly true for *Ane Satyre of the Thrie Estaitis*, since Lindsay wrote a political play which implicitly assumes a knowledge of Scottish politics and the ideas used to order and discuss the political life of the nation. Moreover, Scotland's government took a decisive turn after 1542, with the death of James V shortly after the debacle of Solway Moss when the English once again defeated the Scots. Like the period after the comparable defeat at Flodden Field in 1513, Scotland was left once more with an infant heir and a confused period of government by protectorate, now further complicated by the contortions of the Reformation.

Since the tenor of the nation altered drastically after 1542, the two dates associated with the *Thrie Estaitis*—1540 and 1552—intimately affect potential interpretations of the play's meaning and effect. The soundest evidence supports a first performance near the author's home in Cupar, Fifeshire, on Whitsun Tuesday, June 7, 1552. Yet that evidence, accumulated slowly, has recently been challenged once again with a reading of the play in terms of politics before 1540.[1] Since this is the case, a review of the scholarship on the dating question is more than ritualistic: it is essential, if the subsequent interpretation according to historical materials is to be sound.

The *Thrie Estaitis* survives in two forms, a quarto published in 1602 by Robert Charteris, an Edinburgh printer, and a manuscript copy made by George Bannatyne in 1568. Shorter by nearly 1,600 lines,[2] the latter is a series of extracts from the play and, as such, can provide only an important ancillary to the quarto. It does, however, provide the banns for the play and 52 lines which do not appear in the quarto. The two texts differ in spelling and diction, but these differences have not yet been subjected to linguistic analysis. In general, the Bannatyne seems to preserve more of the Scots dialect while the quarto seems relatively more "southern" in its English. Aside from these linguistic differences, the texts—where they are parallel—do not diverge to any greater extent than that usually found in normal textual problems where the author has had no immediate part in the transmission of his work.[3] The extant texts, then, appear to derive ultimately from one hypothetical authorial manuscript; certainly their differences do not suggest widely variant forms like those, for example, in the three distinct versions of *Piers Plowman*.

If this were the only material available, the chronological problem would be relatively simple, but a further complication exists in the form of a report written to Thomas Cromwell on January 21, 1539/40, by Sir William Eure, English ambassador to Scotland.[4] The report includes notes on an interlude presented at the royal court in Linlithgow on Twelfth-night, 1540. Despite the differences between the report and the texts we possess, this interlude has been associated with Lindsay's play since Eure's letter was first noted in the late eighteenth century. Because the *Thrie Estaitis* is the only Scottish morality play whose text has survived, we have no way of knowing if other plays might fit Eure's description more closely. In any case, the correspondence is close enough that the court interlude may be viewed as a variant on the more complex and rather different play we do possess.

Yet, for all the similarity, considerable difference exists, too. Anna Jean Mill summarizes these differences succinctly, and her account is well worth quoting:

> The summary of the Linlithgow plot as given in the "Nootes" [Eure's report] seems to differ considerably in detail from the plot of the 1602 quarto. In the "Nootes" we have the messenger Solace; in the quarto, Diligence. In the "Nootes" we have the courtiers Placebo, Pikthanke, and Flaterye; in the quarto, Placebo, Wantonness, and Solace. These may be merely verbal changes, and similarly Good Counsall of the

quarto is probably Experience of the "Nootes" under another name. But the speeches of the Poor Man of the "Nootes" have evidently undergone considerable revision; and the character seems to have been extended and duplicated in Pauper and John the Commonweal of the quarto. In the "Nootes" there is no mention of the three Vices, of the Interludes of the Sowtar and Taylor or of the Poorman and the Pardoner, or of the Sermon of Folly. It seems quite clear too that the unmarried King's seduction by Sensualitie, the main theme of Part I in the quarto, did not form part of the Linlithgow plot. "Nexte come in a King," say the "Nootes," "who passed to his throne, having noe speche to th'ende of the Playe (and thene to raitefie and approve as in playne Parliament all things doon by the reste of the players which represented the three estes [estates].)" If, then, the "Nootes" are a faithful summary of the Linlithgow representation, there was considerable variance *in detail* between that and other representations.[5]

The date of 1540 conflicts with other external evidence, too. In four notes, Bannatyne described the play as performed in Edinburgh, during the 1550s, an ascription which agrees with comments by Henrie Charteris in his preface to his 1568 edition of Lindsay's works (exclusive of the *Thrie Estaitis*).[6] This production appears to have been performed on Sunday, August 12, 1554, before the queen-regent, Mary of Lorraine. Yet, in the banns which appear in Bannatyne's manuscript, the heading reads: "Proclamatioun maid in cowpar of ffyffe" and the announcement itself specifies Whitsun Tuesday, June 7, on the Castle Hill at Cupar at 7:00 A.M. as the time and place for the coming performance. While the year is not specified, the range is narrowed by a reference to the battle of Pinkie which occurred on September 10, 1547.[7]

In its simplest form then, the dating argument involves three places and three dates: 1540 in Linlithgow, on the basis of Eure's letter; 1554 in Edinburgh, on the testimony of Bannatyne and Charteris; and 1552 in Cupar, on the basis of the information provided by the banns.[8]

The scholarly discussion of the play's date begins in 1806 with George Chalmer's edition of Lindsay's *Works* where, for the first time since 1602, the complete quarto text was used.[9] The quarto was again edited by Fitzedward Hall for the Early English Text Society (EETS) in 1869 (orig. ser. no. 37). David Laing was responsible for two editions. The first, a popular edition, appeared in 1871, while the second was issued posthumously, with additional work by John Small, in

1879, in a limited edition of 485 copies.[10] The latter is more fully annotated but, according to Douglas Hamer, "the text pages themselves seem to have been printed some years before the appearance of the edition of 1871" (4:111).

The EETS edition includes no further discussion of the date, although the "Fifth Report of the Committee" includes a description of the play as "a most curious sketch of the time, A.D. 1535–9" (p. 12). For all practical purposes, then, the authorities during the nineteenth century were Chalmers and Laing who disagreed in detail if not in substance. While both Chalmers and Laing accept the 1540 document as evidence for the date of the play, they treat its significance differently. Identifying King Humanitie as James V, Chalmers argues that the play must have been written before James's marriage in 1537, since Lindsay's king is unmarried. He denies the relevance of the evidence in the banns and argues for a date of 1535.[11] Laing says that Eure's description does not "materially differ from the play in its printed form." He denies Chalmers's identification of Rex Humanitas with James V and cites Diligence's opening speech (with italics added) as evidence that no such specific identification is included: *"For we shall speik in general* / For pastime and for play." Accepting the evidence of the banns, he sees the 1552 and 1554 performances as occasions when "there may have been numerous changes and alterations which we have no means of ascertaining, by the omission or introduction of short Interludes. But it is obvious, considering the protracted time for the performance, that such Interludes of a coarse and indelicate character were meant for the amusement of the lower classes, during the intervals when the chief auditory had retired for refreshments." [12]

Both editors agree that Eure's report described the *Thrie Estaitis*, although Chalmers saw that performance as subsequent to an earlier form of the play, represented by the 1602 quarto, while Laing views the extant text as possibly a later variant on its original state. Chalmers's argument rests on an assumption that the play literally represents Scottish politics while Laing sees it as a general depiction, not geared to specific personalities of the time. Both editors view the play as a collection of "interludes"—an implicit assumption of fragmentation and lack of real connection between the parts—despite the fact that the sixteenth-century use of the term *interlude* is currently considered vague indeed. Such a view lends itself easily to an assumption that the play is a series of accretions, or added parts, rather than the embodiment of a single concept, executed as one whole; such a view also lends itself easily to a theory of subsequent revisions or expansions of a limited original and is encouraged by the division of the *Thrie Estaitis* into two parts with the second introducing many new characters.[13]

It was not until 1932 that the dating problem was subjected to the analysis of modern scholarship. In her "Representations of Lindsay's *Satyre of the Thrie Estaitis*," [14] Anna Jean Mill examined the arguments and added extensive materials based on research in Scottish records. For its acumen and careful use of evidence, her work must stand as the definitive argument on the dating problem. She carefully demolishes Chalmers's argument, points out further probable allusions to events from 1545–50, and carefully decides that the extant version must be dated 1552: "In the absence of further evidence, therefore, 1552 should be regarded as the date of the first and only performance of the *Satyre of the Thrie Estaitis* at Cupar" (p. 645). On the subject of earlier performances, she is cautious: "There is nowhere any direct reference to Lyndsay, but the general correspondence of the 'Nootes' [Eure's report in 1540] with the plot of Charteris's quarto text, together with Lyndsay's close court connection, has preserved his authorship from challenge" (p. 636).[15] With Mill's article, then, it was established that 1552 is the date represented by the extant text.

This seems clear and simple enough, once one has examined the arguments, and, one would think, the issue should have been settled there, barring some further discovery of contradictory evidence. Yet, in 1936, the forth volume of Hamer's edition of Lindsay appeared, and the waters were muddied once more. Given two texts and Eure's "Nootes," Hamer postulated three versions of the play and had so labelled his reprints of the materials in volume 2, which had appeared in 1931, the year before Mill's article. Thus, the reported 1540 performance was described as "Version I" of the *Thrie Estaitis*, the Bannatyne manuscript is labelled "Version II," and "Version III" is represented by the 1602 quarto (2:1, 8,9). While this 1931 arrangement looks like the simple human tendency to invent three categories for three pieces of evidence, Hamer, in volume 4 (1936), discusses Versions II and III together and states that "despite a trace of revision undertaken for the Edinburgh performance (note to lines 3609–80), I think that most of the gaps in the *Bann. MS.* are due, not to additions made for the 1554 performance, but to deliberate omissions by Bannatyne" (4:134). Such a minor trace of revision would seem to con-

tradict the hypothesis of Versions II and III, but the terms are maintained in a confusing discussion of the date which adds little to Mill's
clearer exposition and research.[16] In 1940, Raymond A. Houk[17] dis-
posed of the "trace of revision" theory by subjecting lines 3609–80 of
the two texts to a comparison which found that the differences could
be explained by Bannatyne's methods of omission.

Thus, by 1940, scholarly opinion had accumulated to support a
date of 1552 for the extant texts and an unchallenged date of 1540
for an earlier version which does not exist in any text. Yet this apparent clarity continues to appear in confused forms whenever the *Thrie
Estaitis* is discussed in histories, and one can find the play read as a
reflection of events in 1540, in 1552, or in 1554, depending on the
focus of the writer.[18] It would seem that most writers rely on Hamer's
discussion and that his three versions continue, despite their
hypothetical nature. Chalmers's identification of Rex Humanitas with
James V has persisted, too, despite Laing's counter argument and
despite the absence of any new evidence to prove such an exclusive
identification.

The latest variation on Chalmers's view appears in an article
where John MacQueen asserts that "the present form of the play
belongs in its essentials to the thirties, even the twenties, rather than
the fifties of the sixteenth century." [19] MacQueen explains the 1552
date as a revival, and for 1540, observes that "if [Eure's] summary is to
be trusted, the text used at the performance was only generally similar to the one which has survived" (p. 135). It is, perhaps, unnecessary
to argue against MacQueen's view in detail, for his remarks on the
dating question are only one part of an essay which also discusses the
questions of text, staging, and satiric effect. One should observe,
however, that his argument is essentially more sophisticated than
Chalmers's, for MacQueen bases his identification of the king in the
play and the king of Scotland on the texts from earlier poems—the
Dreme (1528) and the *Complaynt* (1529–30) where Lindsay did indeed
discuss James V and from which he extracted passages for use in the
play.[20] Yet he dismisses Lindsay's comparable use of materials from
the *Monarche* (written before 1553)[21] in a footnote (p. 141, n. 16),
seems unaware of Houk's correction of Hamer's theory of variant
versions of the texts, ignores the evidence of the banns, and neglects
to account for the two specific references to the date at the end of the
play.

These references occur in a passage within Folly's mock sermon
which ends the play. According to Mill, the first seems to allude to

"the events of the years 1545 to 1550, the period of the Hertford
invasions of Scotland . . . [and] the repeated dispatch of French ships
to the aid of the Scots":[22]

> Quhat cummer haue ȝe had in Scotland
> Be our auld enemies of Ingland?
> Had nocht bene the support of France,
> We had bene brocht to great mischance.

(Ll. 4564–67)

Hamer agrees with the Mill interpretation of this passage and describes it as "the sole internal reference to contemporary events which
can be dated, apart from the references to Pinkie Cleuch, 10th September 1547, in the Cupar Banns" (4:238, ll. 4564–67 n.). But he
rejects her reading of the succeeding lines (ll. 4568–79) as a reference to events in "the last stage of the Smalkaldic war, which ended in
August, 1552, with the peace of Passau" (Mill, "Representations of
Lyndsay's *Satyre*," p. 641). In discussing this second passage which,
like the first, has a parallel in the *Monarche*, Hamer rejects such an
interpretation. For him, Lindsay is simply expressing a general disap-
proval of "the frequency of the wars" which involved the papacy and
the European powers.[23]

To this evidence, however, we may now add a third contemporary
allusion which appears in both the Bannatyne manuscript and in the
1602 quarto. The parallel between lines 4601–8 of the *Thrie Estaitis*
and John Foxe's account of the Pater Noster controversy in *Acts and
Monuments* provides new evidence for dating the play not earlier than
late 1549. Considered with other probable interpretations, the reference supports Mill's conclusion that the extant text was written shortly
before its 1552 performance at Cupar. Although the parallel with
Foxe was noted by two nineteenth-century church historians, their
brief comments have escaped the attention of Lindsay scholars. Yet
Lindsay's reference to the Pater Noster is important because it adds
another element in the text proper (exclusive of the banns) which can
be dated with some precision.

The pertinent lines occur in the play's last speech. Having given
his mock prophecy at the end of a long attack on church and state,
Folie turns his satire back on a specific clerical quarrel:

> So be this prophecy planely it appeiris
> that mortall weir salbe amang the freiris
> That thay sall not weill knaw in to thair cloisteris

to Quhome þat thay sall say thair pater nosteris
Wald thay fall to and fecht with speir & scheild
the Divill mak cair quhilk of thame tynt the feild
(Ll. 335–40, Bannatyne MS)[24]

Sa be this Prophesie plainlie appeirs,
That mortall weirs salbe amang freirs:
Thay sall nocht knaw weill in thair closters,
To quhom thay sall say thair Pater nosters.
Wald thay fall to, and fecht with speir and sheild,
The feind mak cuir quhilk of them win the feild.
(Ll. 4601–8, 1602 quarto)

The reference is to an event in Scotland first described by Foxe in the
1570 edition of *Acts and Monuments*.[25] It seems that an Englishman
named Richard Marshall had preached a sermon at Saint Andrews
asserting that the Pater Noster should be addressed only to God.
Having been taught that they might also address the prayer to saints,
the people responded to the new idea with confusion, and, Foxe
continues, on All Saints' Day, 1551, a certain Friar Toittis attempted
to argue in a public sermon that the Pater Noster might also be said to
the saints. But the friar's attempt to fit his argument to the text for the
day (Matt. 5) became so obviously strained that the sermon intensified
public ridicule and clerical quarrel. Eventually, the matter was settled
in a provincial council of the church, but while the controversy raged,
pasquils mysteriously appeared on the walls of Saint Andrews Abbey
Church. Foxe prints one lampoon in English which contains the same
rhymes that Lindsay employed in lines 4601–4:

Doctors of Theologie, of foure score of yeares,
And Old iolye Lupoys the balde gray Friers,
They would be called *Rabbi* and *Magister noster*,
And wot not to whom they say their Pater noster.

If Foxe's account is correct, the performance at Cupar on June 7
ended with a biting effect. Six months before, in January, the Provincial Council of the Scottish Catholic Church had met in Edinburgh
and had finally authorized the production of the catechism which
would end the dispute. In June, that book was not yet printed; when it
finally did appear the author simply said that the Pater Noster was to
be said to God and kept silent on the subject of the saints.[26] In June,
the audience was probably still savoring the comic discomfort of the

conservative clergy at a religious quarrel which ended in a small victory for the left wing of Christendom: the prayer was to be presented in the vernacular, and the *Our Father* was restored to its rightful recipient, God alone. If we accept Foxe's dates, Lindsay must have been working on the play and have finished it sometime between November 1, 1551, when the controversy erupted publicly, and early June, 1552, when the play had its first performance.

As it sometimes does, however, modern scholarship complicated this simple chronology and raised a small controversy of its own. During the nineteenth century, dominant scholarly opinion characterized John Foxe as a fanatic Protestant given to gross exaggeration and, as such, an untrustworthy historian.[27] Since Foxe's account of the Pater Noster controversy is the only one known, opinion generally held that such a ridiculous event could not possibly have occurred and that Foxe printed the story as a mere polemic against the Papists. As a result, Joseph Robertson avoided the sensible conclusion when, in 1866, he pointed out Lindsay's reference to the Pater Noster incident. In a note to his edition of the *Statua Ecclesiae Scoticanae*, Robertson followed the historian Grubbe's opinion that the incident, as reported by Foxe, could not have happened, and then decided that Lindsay's apparently supporting testimonial to Foxe's veracity possibly referred to "some such question [as] may have been mooted in some convent of the Mendicant Orders."[28] While not directly contradicting his colleagues nor mentioning their names, Alexander F. Mitchell answered each of Grubbe's and Robertson's objections in his introduction to the 1882 edition of *Hamilton's Catechism and the Two Penny Faith*.[29] Since it is now ninety years later, one may argue frankly that Foxe's account glosses Lindsay's lines and that Lindsay's lines bear witness to Foxe's narrative.

Clearly, Robertson's suggestion of a minor dispute within "some cloister" has no evidence behind it at all and would never have been raised if *Acts and Monuments* had not suffered a nineteenth-century decline. Since then, Foxe's reputation has been vindicated by J. F. Mozley, who convincingly demonstrates that the historian was a careful reporter, within the limits of human error.[30] As with all writers, however, one cannot unquestioningly accept Foxe's every detail. But, once we take his account seriously, the problem then becomes one of checking Foxe's facts, and it is here that complexities arise. Following his custom with the Scots material, Foxe labels the Pater Noster story *ex testemonio e Scotia allato*. The report was first published in 1570 when *Acts and Monuments* was greatly expanded over its first English edition (1563) by the addition of new research and new material with which enthusiastic readers had showered Foxe.[31] It is possible, then, that Foxe's Scots source for the Pater Noster story sent him a manuscript account, and the original possibly may exist still.[32] Since we do not know Foxe's source precisely, however, we cannot estimate the informant's accuracy nor the time at which he recalled the events. He might have assembled the information for Foxe sometime between 1563 and 1570, or the account may have been produced in the 1550s and later sent to Foxe as an interesting recollection. Without this hypothetical manuscript—or perhaps even with it—we cannot know the informant's qualifications.

Without its source, Foxe's published text provides our only clues, and his report does not lack corroborating evidence. As Mitchell observed, an incomplete canon remains in the Provincial Council's decrees of November 27, 1549.[33] The entire passage reads: "Circa Orationem Dominicam *Pater Noster*, etc. Concilium decrevit ex moventibus hoc vulgare quod sequitur his inserendum," and, after a lacuna, the next passage commands that "in omnium concionum publicarum exordiis servetur vetus et receptus invocandi modus per Orationem Dominicam, cum Salutatione Angelica ad Virginem Deiparam, pro gratis impetranda."[34] In other words, a decree concerning the Lord's Prayer was apparently considered and judgment deferred, while the following section provides for public prayer according to the ancient and received form. The next conciliar decrees, issued on January 26, 1551/52, endorsed and described a prospective catechism in the vernacular: "quem Cathechismum, id est, communem et facilem rudimentorum fidei institutionem et doctrinam vocari vult . . . continentem veram sinceramque, juxta Catholicae ecclesiae sensum ac intellectum decem mandatorum Dei interpretationem, articulorum fidei, septemque sacramentorum simplicem, puram et Christianam doctrinam, nec non Orationis Dominicae et Salutationis Angelicae integram et salutarem expositionem."[35] From the lacuna in the decrees of 1549 and the order for the catechism in 1552, it appears certain that some discussion of the Pater Noster began on or before November 27, 1549, and was resolved on January 26, 1551/52. That much is clear.

But could the preliminary events described by Foxe have occurred before November 26, 1549, and added fuel to the controversy which occurred in the council, or might the public manifestations have happened in the intervening two years when the issue may have grown to such proportions that the church hastened to compromise in 1552? Foxe mentions three names in his account: "Richard Mershall Doctour of Divinitie and Priour of the Blacke Friers at the new Castle in England," [36] a Friar Toittis, and a Friar Scott. Two of the names appear in the list of participants in the council of 1549. "Frater Joannes Scott" is listed under the heading "Ordines Minorum de Observantia," and under "Doctores in Theologia, Licentiati et Baccalaurei," the name of "Frater Richardus Marchell, Anglus, Divinarum Litterarum professor," appears. In addition, a "Frater Andreas Cottis" is described as the guardian of the Friars Minor Observants at Saint Andrews. [37] The similarity between the name Cottis and Toittis added to the fact that the former was at Saint Andrews leads one to suspect that it was Andrew Cottis who preached the exaggerated sermon on All Saints' Day and that the name Toittis in the 1570 edition of *Acts and Monuments* is probably an editorial error that has continued to the present. Thus far, Foxe's facts are accurate. There was some sort of disagreement about the Pater Noster in Scotland during the period 1549–52, and the three men Foxe mentions were indeed present at the council in 1549. Lindsay's lines, echoing the rhyme Foxe quotes, must refer to the local controversy which either promoted or was incited by a similar disagreement at the conciliar session of 1549. From Foxe's account, the incident seems to have occurred in November, 1551, just before the final decision was made in the following January.

Lindsay's reference to the Pater Noster dispute provides external evidence which limits the date for *Ane Satyre* and reduces the time span suggested by the only other references which have been identified heretofore. These are the mention of Pinckie, 1547, in the banns, and the apparent reference to the French army's presence in Scotland during 1548–50 (lines 4564–67). Taking the latter, with the Pater Noster reference, it then seems consistent to read lines 4568–79 ("Now I heir tell the Empreour, / Schaippis for till be ane Conqueror . . .") as a description of the continental war of 1551–52. This is the interpretation proposed by Mill, and despite Hamer's rejection of it, the contemporary character of the other events, taken with the Pater Noster reference, makes such an interpretation probable. The final citation, "Sanct Peter, Sanct Paull nor Sanct Androw, / Raisit never sic ane Oist I trow" (lines 4580–81), may be read as a reference to the year-long seige of Saint Andrews during 1546 and 1547. Considering these events together, we see that Folie ends his sermon by attacking the specific manifestations of national folly: the English invasion of

Scotland; the war involving the pope, Charles V, and Henry II of France; the internal Scottish assault on Saint Andrews; and, finally, the current Fifeshire folly—the Pater Noster quarrel.

But if the most conservative limits for the extant version of the *Thrie Estaitis* are 1549–52, what are we to say about the description of 1540? It is difficult to argue about the nature of a text which does not exist, and especially so when we are working with a play which we cannot surround with the texts of contemporary dramatic productions that we know, from records, did indeed occur.[38] Certainly, Eure's notes represent a piece of evidence, but their relevance seems largely a function of one's view of the text we do possess. Laing emphasizes the similarities between the report and the text; Chalmers and MacQueen emphasize the differences. Yet both Chalmers and Laing see the play as a collection of interludes, i.e., related fragments, a view which permits one to argue that a 1540 version subsequent to that produced in the 1530s must have been an extract (Chalmers) or that a 1540 production provided the basis for a later revision (Laing, Hamer). Yet the fact remains that we have only one text which, if the 1540 notes did not exist, would provide sound evidence for dating it 1551–52. Moreover, if one views the drama as an artistic whole, then the theory of accretion of parts becomes irrelevent. This study, I believe, demonstrates that artistic unity and argues that the apparent shifts in the play's action are the result of a dramaturgy which proceeds by a demonstration of theme, rather than by the later method which centers its unity on the exposition of a protagonist's action.

If this approach is indeed sound, then we must take another view of Eure's notes, a view which is at least plausible from our knowledge of the practice of modern writers. While it is true that Eure's account, in general, sounds like Lindsay's play, the differences in the characters' names and in the scope of the action suggests a very different play indeed. While there is no evidence that he did, Lindsay may have written such an entertainment for the court at Linlithgow in 1540, or, if we possessed other examples of contemporary Scottish plays connected with the court, we might be better able to evaluate the possibility that the 1540 performance was indeed produced by Lindsay and not by any of the other writers who were also part of the Scottish literary world. Unfortunately, we simply do not know.

Even assuming that Eure is indeed reporting Lindsay's work, we should use the term *Version I* cautiously. James Joyce, after all, wrote an earlier version of *Portrait of the Artist as a Young Man*, just as Proust wrote an earlier version of *Remembrance of Things Past*. Yet, valuable as they are for studying the growth of the final masterwork, we do not confuse *Stephen Hero* or *Jean Santeuil* with the later work when undertaking a critical study of the texts for which their writers are valued and remembered.

Taken in this light, it is neither sensible nor logical to discuss a text we do have on the basis of a hypothetical text which might or might not have been close enough to the *Thrie Estaitis* to be labeled Version I. We have only one text of *Ane Satyre of the Thrie Estaitis*, and it exists in two forms: one, Anglicized and complete; the other, Scots and incomplete. Considering the Pater Noster reference alone, we should date the play, conservatively, 1549–52. Within its context, lines 4568–79 seem more likely to refer to the European war of 1551–52. If we accept the latter interpretation and Foxe's date of 1551, *Ane Satyre of the Thrie Estaitis* must have been written sometime between the end of 1551 and its performance on June 7, 1552. A counterargument could hold that these contemporary references were added only for the Cupar performance, but this would seem to push the accretion theory beyond the bounds of common sense, since the materials for the 1552 date are specific while the evidence of Eure's report is only, at the very most, possible evidence for a not-impossible earlier draft. In any case, we simply cannot tell, for we have only one text.

The choice between 1540 and 1552 for the date of Lindsay's play is not simply a matter of arguing for a historical record of approximate accuracy. The decision determines both how far we extend the historical limits of the time to which the play refers, and, given those limits, how we may apply the materials of history in an attempt to describe the meaning of the dramatic action. No one has directly challenged the 1540 date, but it remains an impediment to interpretation. As Anna Jean Mill observed in 1932, "there is nowhere any direct reference to Lyndsay, but the general correspondence of the 'Nootes' [Eure's report in 1540] with the plot of Charteris's quarto text [1602], together with Lyndsay's close court connection, has preserved his authorship from challenge." [39] Any attempt to interpret the play in light of its relevance to Scottish affairs must accept that challenge. If other versions indeed existed, we do not have them. If the *Thrie Estaitis* should be interpreted solely in terms of events before 1540, we must have factual evidence as solid as that for the later date. Such evidence, so far, has not emerged. For our purposes, then, we shall disregard Eure's report and take as our reference point the performance for which the surviving text itself provides unmistakable evidence: June 7, 1552.

NOTES

1. See John MacQueen, "Ane Satyre of the Thrie Estaitis," *Studies in Scottish Literature 3* (1966): 129–43, and the rebuttal by Anna Jean Mill, "The Original Version of Lindsay's *Satyre of the Thrie Estaitis*," ibid. 6 (1968): 67–75. Also, Vernon Harward, *"Ane Satyre of the Thrie Estaitis* Again," ibid. 7 (1970): 139–46.

2. James Kinsley, "Note on the Text," in his edition of *Ane Satyre of the Thrie Estaitis* (London: Cassell, 1954), p. 36.

3. Cf. the variants listed in vol. 4, 132–35 of the standard edition of Lindsay's works, edited by Douglas Hamer for the Scottish Text Society, 4 vols. (Edinburgh: William Blackwood and Sons, 1931–36), and in Kinsley's edition, pp. 35–37, 199–201. Since Lindsay died in 1555, both versions were done after his death.

4. Brit. Mus. MS Reg. 7. C. xvi. fols. 137–39 printed in Hamer edition of *Works*, 2:2–6 with commentary in 4:125–26. A reprint of Hamer's text appears here in the Appendix.

5. Anna Jean Mill, "Representations of Lyndsay's *Satyre of the Thrie Estaitis*," *PMLA* 47 (1932): 644.

6. See Hamer, ed., *Works*, 4:139–43, and A. J. Mill's *Medieval Plays in Scotland*, Saint Andrews University Publications, no. 24 (Edinburgh: William Blackwood and Sons, 1927), pp. 181–82.

7. Hamer, ed., *Works*, 2: 10, 20; ll. 125 and 139.

8. The argument for the latter two dates are specifically set forth by Mill in "Representations of Lyndsay's *Satyre*," although Laing also lists them (without evidence) in his 2-volume (Edinburgh, 1871) edition of Lindsay's *Poetical Works*, 2 xxxiv, as "subsequent performances" of the play.

9. The Bannatyne text was earlier printed by Pinkerton in 1788. Sibbald printed excerpts from the quarto (rearranged into five "acts") in two issues in 1802. The entire Bannatyne manuscript was printed by the Hunterian Club in 4 vols., (Glasgow, 1873–1900), and, in the standard edition, by the Scottish Text Society, 4 vols. (Edinburgh, 1928–33). See Hamer, ed., *Works*, 4:130–31.

10. Hamer, ed., *Works*, 4:106–11.

11. See Mill, "Representations of Lindsay's *Satyre*," pp. 641–45, for a detailed exposition and rebuttal of Chalmers's views. Besides the announcement of time and place, the banns include a short dramatic sketch; the characters and action are not related to the play itself.

12. Laing, ed., *Works*, (1871), 1:xxxiii–xxxv. Laing recognized that the 1602 quarto does not break the play into interludes or parts of any kind, yet in printing the text he separates the parts which he thinks "interrupt the progress of the play" (see 2:347–48, 351).

13. The analysis subsequently presented here argues that the play provides a unity of concept with a two-part division in emphasis and dramatic technique.

14. Mill, "Representations of Lyndsay's *Satyre*," pp. 636–51.

15.. John Row (born 1568) in a history written ca. 1625, refers to a fourth performance given at Perth before James V. Mill finds little evidence for this and cites Laing's observation that "Row may have substituted the name of St. Johnston (Perth) for that of Linlithgow (the site of the 1540 performance)." She further adds that "Laing's suspicions, one is forced to admit, may be justified" (see ibid., 645–47). Hamer connects Row's statements with a traditional connection between James V and Lindsay (see *Works*, 4:156, 157).

16. Still, Hamer's editing task included many more problems to solve than this one; with its wealth of materials, the four-volume edition is immensely valuable.

17. R. A. Houk, "Versions of Lindsay's *Satire of the Three Estates*," *PMLA* 55 (1940): 396–405.

18. For example, compare the dates used by different authors in *Essays on the Scottish Reformation*, ed. David McRoberts (Glasgow: Burns, 1962), pp. 75, 173, 470. These examples can be multiplied many times over in both literary and historical books. A. M. Kinghorn uses "the 1530s" in his discussion of Lindsay's work, chapter 9, in *The Chorus of History and Literature—Historical Relations in Renaissance Britain* (New York: Barnes and Noble, 1971).

19. MacQueen, "Ane Satyre of the Thrie Estaitis," p. 136. In his most recent reference to the play, MacQueen dates it "in or about 1535" but says it was "not certainly performed until 1552" (*Allegory* [London: Methuen, 1970], p. 72).

20. I discuss these passages in chapter 2.

21. See Hamer's discussion of the date of the *Monarche*, in *Works*, 3:237–38.

22. Mill, "Representations of Lyndsay's *Satyre*," p. 640.

23. See Hamer, ed., *Works*, 4:238, ll. 4568–89 note and also 222, ll. 3562–63 note. Here, Diligence remarks that "Thay se the Paip with awfull ordinance / Makis weir against the michtie King of France." This occurs just after the examination of the clergy in part 2. The lines are paralleled in the *Monarche* which was published in late 1552 or early 1553 (Hamer, ed., *Works*, 3:237–38).

24. *The Bannatyne Manuscript*, ed. W. Tod Ritchie, Vol. 3, Scottish Text Society (Edinburgh: William Blackwood and Sons, 1928), p. 163. One should read the Bannatyne MS text in its original order, since Hamer rearranged some passages to parallel the quarto text.

25. All quotations are from the Folger Library copy of *Acts and Monuments*, 1570 edition, pp. 1450–52. For convenience, one must resort to the inadequate editions in 8 vols. published by Seeley of London from 1853–77, based on S. R. Cattley's edition, revised by Josiah Pratt. There, the Pater Noster account is in vol. 5, pt. 2, pp. 641–44.

W. Murison discusses the reference briefly in his biography, *Sir David Lyndsay* (Cambridge: At the University Press, 1938), pp. 117–19. However, he does not include Foxe's date nor its relevance to the play's date.

26. See *The Cathechism of John Hamilton,* ed. Thomas Graves Law (Oxford: Clarendon Press, 1884), p. 292. The colophon of the catechism is dated August 29, 1552.

27. J. F. Mozley, *John Foxe and His Book* (London: Society for Promoting Christian Knowledge, 1940), pp. 175–203, especially pp. 181–85. V. Norskov Olsen discusses Foxe as a theologian in *John Foxe and the Elizabethan Church* (Berkeley: University of California Press, 1973).

28. J. Robertson, ed., *Ecclesiae Scoticanae Statua Tam Provincialia Quam Synodalia Quae Supersunt MCCXXV–MDLIX,* vol. 2 (Edinburgh: Archibald Constable, 1866), 295, note to p. 121, no. 226. See also 1:cxvii. David Patrick's translation (with new notes) is entitled *Statutes of the Scottish Church, 1225–1559,* Scottish History Society, no. 54 (Edinburgh: Edinburgh University Press, 1907).

29. *Hamilton's Catechism and the Two-Penny Faith* (Edinburgh: William Blackwood and Sons, 1882), pp. xxiii–xxiv.

30. Mozley, *John Foxe and His Book,* pp. 118–241.

31. Ibid., p. 141. The Scottish accounts appear on pp. 1107–17 and pp. 1442–53 of the 1570 edition of *Acts and Monuments.* Foxe's labels vary, suggesting several different sources.

32. I have had a search made of Lansdowne 389 and 819 in the British Museum. This seemed the most likely places for such a document. Unfortunately, the search was unsuccessful.

33. *Hamilton's Catechism,* p. xxxiii.

34. Robertson, ed., *Ecclesiae Scoticanae Statua,* 2:121. Patrick's translation, *Statutes of the Scottish Church,* pp. 127–28: "Concerning the Lord's prayer, 'Our Father' etc. The council enacted, for reasons appealing to it, that this [statement] in the vulgar tongue which follows should be here inserted." The next article is: "Of the 'Our Father' and 'Hail Mary' before sermons. At the beginning of all public sermons the ancient and received form of invocation by saying the Lord's Prayer and the Angelical Salutation to the Virgin Mother of God to obtain grace shall be observed."

35. Robertson, ed., *Ecclesiae Scoticanae Statua,* 2:136. Patrick's translation, *Statutes of the Scottish Church,* p. 144: "which . . . Catechism, that is to say, a plain and easy statement and explanation of the rudiments of the faith . . . having for its contents a true and faithful interpretation of the Decalogue, or Ten Commandments of God, according to the sense and meaning of the Catholic Church, a plain, orthodox, and Christian instruction on the articles of the Creed and the seven sacraments, as also a complete and edifying explanation of the Lord's Prayer and Angelical Salutation." The text continues with a rebuke of ignorant clergymen.

36. John Durkan has traced the career of Richard Marshall, originally a Dominican of Newcastle, in his essay "The Cultural Background in Sixteenth-Century Scotland," in *Essays on the Scottish Reformation,* ed.

McRoberts, pp. 274–31 and especially pp. 326–29. The English exile appears in Scotland in 1539 and apparently joined the faculty of Saint Andrews in 1547. I am grateful to Durkan for correspondence on his research.

37. Robertson, ed., *Ecclesiae Scoticanae Statua*, 2:83, 84.
38. See Mill's *Medieval Plays in Scotland*.
39. Mill, "Representations of Lyndsay's *Satyre*," p. 636.

Chapter 2

History

1526 James V begins personal rule.

1528 The Douglas group is outlawed by James. Patrick Hamilton burned for heresy.

1534 Gourlay and Stratton burned for heresy.

1539 Marriage of James V and Mary of Lorraine. Thomas Forret and four others burned for heresy.

1540 Sir John Borthwick condemned for heresy, but escapes.

1542 The battle of Solway Moss. In December, James V dies. Mary Queen of Scots born. Arran becomes regent.

1543 September, Arran joins the French faction. Mary betrothed to Dauphin and sent to France. This ends the English negotiation for a marriage to Edward VI.

1544 English harrassment of Scotland begins: "The Rough Wooing." Five heretics executed in Perth.

1545 Council of Trent opens.

1546 George Wishart tried and executed. Cardinal Beaton murdered and Saint Andrews occupied by reformers. John Hamilton succeeds Cardinal Beaton.

1547 Scottish appeal for French aid. Henry VIII dies in England. French take reformers at Saint Andrews prisoner in July. In September, the battle of Pinkie. English occupy Haddington.

1549 Pope Paul III dies. First reforming decrees issued from Scottish Provincial Council.

1550 Julius III becomes pope. Adam Wallace burned for heresy. Treaty of Boulogne brings peace between England and France.

1552 January, second decrees from the Scottish Provincial Council which also authorizes a catechism explaining prayers in the vernacular.
June 7, *Ane Satyre of the Thrie Estaitis* performed at Cupar.

The old problem of the relationship between art and actuality has provided endless discussion, amusement, and disagreement for centuries. Again and again, people interested in the arts have asked, how much is the artist dependent on his own experience; how much is his work shaped by his own imagination? While the various answers usually differ primarily in their emphasis of one aspect or the other, the sensible critic must balance on a delicate line, always risking overemphasis of the purely historical or of the purely artistic. When the subject is satire, a term usually associated with mockery of contemporary events,[1] the risk increases, for he may be accused of finding allusions under every metaphor or, conversely, of taking the tale so literally that he misses many of the points and becomes the man at the party who has to have every joke explained to him.

At Cupar in 1552, the people watching Lindsay's play had behind them the vivid political experience of 1526–52. Their memories would be even more intense than our memories of the recent political past, for many of the events happened in an area around Cupar no larger than the environs of some of our cities: James V had frequently sojourned nearby; gentlemen from Fife were prominent in the court; throughout the period, heretics were tried at Saint Andrews, less than ten miles away; rebels held the castle in 1546–47 for more than a year; the English had attempted to invade Fife in 1548. It is unlikely that *Ane Satyre of the Thrie Estaitis* was, for sixteenth-century Scots, a mere attack on general evils; the issues of the play are the issues of their time, and men generalize only after they think of particulars. Certainly, George Bannatyne understood it as such when in 1568 he copied out amusing parts of the play and omitted "the grave mater thairof becaws the samyne abuse Is weill reformit in scotland." [2] More explicit in a later section, he described the play as "maid . . . to the mocking of abusionis usit in the cuntre by diverss sortis of Estait." [3]

Yet, while the play *is* firmly set in contemporary Scottish experience, it yields little specific reference and proceeds instead by the invention of parallel and generalized action. This is exactly what Lindsay says in the opening speech of the play: "Tak na man greif in speciall / For wee sall speik in generall." Although this may be called a conventional disavowal of specific attack, study of Scottish history yields no specific identifications and thus no contradiction of the view that Lindsay does what he says. What history does yield is a set of probable parallels which heighten and give point to the general situations depicted in the play.

Even the identification of James V with Rex Humanitas, the fictional king of the play, is not unshakable. That identification rests on the evidence of Lindsay's *Complaynt* (1529–30), a poem specifically addressed to James V and clearly relevent to the political situation then current. Yet, reading the play in general terms, one can also parallel the behavior of Rex Humanitas with the later, disappointing performance of the regent, the duke of Arran, who also fell under the influence of interfering clergymen after an auspicious beginning as a governor. This second association becomes possible when one investigates the struggles centered around the accusations of heresy which culminated with the execution of George Wishart in 1546 and the subsequent assassination of David Cardinal Beaton. With this later material, one sees a shift in emphasis from the kingdom depicted in the *Complaynt*, where the courtiers are held responsible for the realm's misgovernment, to a view which presents mock clergymen attempting to hold power through accusations of heresy. Such a shift in emphasis is consistent with the political tone of 1552.

The history recounted here, then, begins with 1526 because that is the date when the regency for the boy-king passed into the Douglas power. (James V's father had died at Flodden Field in 1513.) The date is merely a convenience, for what we are attempting to sketch is a brief view of the man and his reign in order to connect it with the events that followed, under the Regency of Arran (1542–54). If we take the view that the characters and situations are generalizations based on historical agents and events, we must attempt to reconstruct the elements within the political consciousness of that Cupar audience in 1552. The memory of most generations easily stretches back twenty-five years, and it is approximately that span of time which our account covers.

The major sources of this account are biased materials deliberately selected because they represent the point of view which Lindsay and a sympathetic audience were likely to share. Fortunately, Lindsay, as a writer, stands in a rather curious relation to the historians of his time. In his role as first herald of Scotland, he was, like Milton, an observer and minor participant in the great events of his nation. As Lion Herald, he appears in English reports as a man on the fringe of events, escorting Sir Ralph Sadler, the diplomat, on his official calls in February, 1539,[4] delivering messages to the Privy Council and, perhaps, being exiled from court in 1543 in a move against the reformer's faction.[5] He himself has left us the only eyewitness account

of James V's early life in his *Complaynt*, and a study of his role as
political propagandist would include most of his extant work:
*Testament of the Papyngo, The Tragedie of the Late Cardinal Beaton, The
Thrie Estaitis*, and *The Monarche*. In addition, the voice of his faction is
well represented by two of his associates, Pitscottie and Knox. Robert
Lindsay of Pitscottie was a much younger contemporary and distant
relative of David Lindsay.[6] Whether Pitscottie gathered the material
for his history informally or from written sources, he cites Sir David as
one of his nine authorities. Of the other eight, all but one—John
Major, the scholar of Saint Andrews—were gentlemen of Fife, and
thus, it is logical to expect, the *Chronicles* are implicitly a Fifeshire
record of Scotland.[7] The other, and greater, historian is, of course,
John Knox, and Lindsay's connection with him is minor, but definite.
On a Sunday shortly after Easter, 1547, the great reformer was encouraged to become a preacher by John Rough, formerly Arran's
chaplin, Henry Balnaves, a prominent reformer, and Sir David
Lindsay.[8]

Pitscottie and Knox. Our major sources. One of them a Lindsay
himself and a Fifeshire man; the other, a reformer and, in later years,
the leader of the faction which drew a good part of its political and
spiritual strength from Lindsay's locale.[9] History has left us more
than we might hope for as a key to the attitudes of that audience at
Cupar on June 7, 1552.

For this is a matter where the "truth" of history is not an issue: the
historian's canon of objective interpretation is not our concern. We do
not need to know what forces really produced a particular event or
what the motives of adversaries really were. We do not even have to
be careful not to develop preferences. As the audience of this play, we
are protestants, not as yet fixed in our separate factions, but united in
our opposition to moral wrongs and papistical adversaries. We believe
the state is infested with ignorant and licentious churchmen, and that
the church, perverted by centuries of neglect and mired in pagan
tradition and worldly goods, must be cleansed and re-formed in the
image of the New Testament. On the Bible's evidence, we believe that
God is directly and personally involved in our national history and
that the scourge of his correction is seen on the land. As literary
critics, we are not concerned with the truth or error of this view. Our
interest is not what really happened, but what the Cupar audience was
likely to think had happened. We are aware that historians regard
Pitscottie as untrustworthy but imaginative and charming. We know

that while Knox's history "stands up well to the tests of modern research, and . . . is vital for any study of his time," [10] he is frequently less than charitable. But we are interested in the passions of our faction as well as their deeds, and, for that, the Catholic Bishop John Leslie's *History of Scotland* is of little value.

With the historians as guides, we must first decide what sort of event Lindsay used as "raw material" in order to identify and describe the response of the play's ideal audience. I propose, then, that we regard the *Thrie Estaitis* as an account of Scots history from 1526 to 1552.[11] It is true that Diligence speaks the conventional disavowal of specific attack:

> Prudent peopill, I pray ʒow all,
> Tak na man greif in speciall:
> For wee sall speik in generall,
> For pastyme and for play.

> (Ll. 70–73)[12]

But the warning is wise, for the action of the play begins with a parallel to James V's reign, earlier presented in Lindsay's *Complaynt*, and in the *Dreme*. In 1526, Archibald, earl of Angus, helped by the earlier maneuvers of James V's mother, Margaret Tudor, gained control of the kingdom by a simple power play.[13] The twelve-year-old king had been declared of age to rule in 1524, and the council of four nobles appointed in 1525 to help him govern was soon undermined by the Douglases with their family leader, the earl of Angus, as the chief administrator. To keep the boy-king docile, his caretakers indulged his every whim and introduced him to new pleasures. With James in their power, the Douglases proceeded to personal gain, laying up their family treasures through benefices and bribes until finally, in 1528, the young king escaped and sent his former keepers into an exile that lasted until his death in December, 1542.

Surely it is no accident that Lindsay told a comparable tale in the *Thrie Estaitis*. Not only is the general outline of the young king's seduction the same as it is in the *Complaynt*, but whole lines, and in one case, a long exchange, are taken from the poem and inserted into appropriate places in the play. In the poem, Lindsay tells us that the courtiers placated James when

> Sum gart hym raiffell at the rakcat;
> Sum harld hym to the hurly hakcat;

And sum, to schaw thare courtlie corsis,
Wald ryid to leith, and try thare horssis,
And wychtle wallope ouer the sandis.

(Ll. 175–79)

In the play, the courtiers similarly distract King Humanitie's attention when, by chance, he sees Gude-Counsall. Wantoness tells him

Better go reuell at the rackat,
Or ellis go to the hurlie hackat,
Or then to schaw our curtlie corsses,
Ga se quha best can rin thair horsses.

(Ll. 1020–23)

But the order of seduction is changed in the play, and the introduction of the ladies takes precedence over other sports. As in the poem, the courtiers, with their superior knowledge, play on the young king's lusts. With James V, the men had more than one suggestion, but the passage from the *Complaynt* begins in a direct manner:

Quode ane: the Deuyll stik me with ane knyfe.
Bot, schir, I knaw ane maid in fyfe,
Ane of the lusteast wantoun lassis,
Quhare to, schir, be gods blude scho passis

(Ll. 237–40)

While, in the *Thrie Estaitis*, Solace makes his suggestion in a gentler fashion:

Sir I have sene I ȝow assure,
The fairest earthlie creature,
That ever was formit be nature
And maist for to advance

(Ll. 194–97)

and continues to describe Sensualitie's physical embellishments. Finally, a long section of the *Complaynt* (lines 186–214) appears, with the slightest of changes, in the play (lines 984–1009). In the poem, the conspiracy to steal from James is formed by a character named Schir Flattre, while in the play, the Vices as mock clergymen perfect their plot with the same words.

The shift in order and emphasis suggests that one should not take

Lindsay's *Complaynt* as a literal key to the opening action of the *Thrie Estaitis*. The effort would result in chaos: should we identify the Douglases with the courtiers or with the Vices, and who would be the likely candidate for the group left over? Moreover, by 1552 James had been dead for ten years; the national situation was quite different; and we know from references in the play that incidents later than 1542 also contribute to the satire. Certainly, the child, Mary of Scotland, is completely outside the scope of the play. Arran, the regent, may be a likely candidate, but for different reasons, as we shall see later. But something happened to James between 1528 and 1542, and to the realm as a result.

If we move away from literal considerations, we may find another approach. At the end of the *Complaynt*, written around 1529 or 1530,[14] Lindsay urged his sovereign to reform the clergy. He tells him current religious abuses are "aganis the lordis command" and admonishes James:

> I do thy grace tyll vnderstand,
> Geue thow to mennis lawis assent,
> Aganis the lordis commandiment,
> As Ieroboam and mony mo,
> Prencis of Israell, allso,
> Assentaris to Ydolatrie,
> Quhilkis puneist was rycht pieteouslie,
> And from thare realmes wer rutit oute,
> So sall thow be, withouttin doute
>
> (Ll. 424–32)

And so it happened. Like so many Scots kings before him, James V died young, leaving an infant heir. And the old game of Scots politics and power began again after a brief respite of fourteen years.

As a person, James was well loved, and time has not yet obliterated his fond title, "the poor man's king." In his brief maturity, he controlled the border thieves, quelled the fierce highlanders, and attempted to establish an effective system for distributing justice to all. He set his own estates in feu, developed herds of sheep and cattle, and even, at times, admonished the clergy to reform[15] while at the same time working to shift some of the church's wealth into the royal treasury. But one policy in particular, his support of the pope and the established order in religion, coupled with his failure to force any means of reformation, turned the loyalties of a growing faction against him. Despite his graces—and they were many—James V, for Lindsay's liberal faction, ultimately symbolized the power of the status quo which answered the protesting cry for reform with heresy trials. As a result, personal faults which might have passed unnoticed in another era became the explanation for his downfall. In a fashion more temperate than the colorful Knox, Pitscottie summarizes the reformers' view of their King:

> This nobill prince, gif he had ressàwit goode consall of wyse and godlie men and spetiallie of his great lordis and keipit his body frome harlotrie and had left the evill consall of his papistis bischopis and gredie cour- teouris, he had ben the most nobillist prince that ever rang in the realme of Scotland. Ffor he was full of pollacie and honestie in his beginning and did money goode actis in his realme. . . . Bot . . . he was abussit witht papistrie and wald nocht suffer the worde of god to haue frie passage in his realme. . . . Ane wther cause thair was, the great profeit that the bischopis gaif of him to be the popis man and to defend his autorietie and the kirkmens libertie that he, abussit throw covettous- ness, consentit to thair wickit and evill consall agains the evangell of Jesus Christ quhilk was the principall caus of his ewill success in his latter dayis. Ffor the bischopis and preistis and freiris seand that they could not haue better nor be flatterie they wnderstude that he might tak his pleasour throw all Scotland and they him cheise any of quhat gen- tillwoman he pleissit, quhither they war marieit or unmarieit and sa to spend his body wupon thame as he pleissit contrair the command of God. Ffor they pat him in sic beleif that they suld mak sic spetiall paperis for him that god sould nocht be movit witht him so he wsit thair consall and defendit the libertie of hollie kirk. So they gart him both wse idolatrie and adulltterie, idolatrie in stopping of Christis evangell, adull- tierie in using of uther mens wyffis. Fo they abusit this nobill prince that he tint the favour of god and the nobillis of his realme, quhairthrow he tuik great displesour and melancolie, quhairby he was constranit and stranglit to the deid.[16]

The double charge of lechery and avarice ring out again in the writings of David Lindsay himself, of Knox, of George Buchanan, and even in the more contemporary sources of Sadler's diplomatic reports and in a conversation conveyed in an official letter of 1541 by Sir Thomas Wharton, border officer for Henry VIII.[17] Nor, indeed, does one have to search far for evidence to support the generaliza- tions of our faction. From November 5, 1534, to July 3, 1541, James directed a series of letters to the pope asking, and securing, five of the best benefices for his four illegitimate sons who ranged from five to twelve years old at the time they entered upon their offices and their incomes.[18] All together, we know of five royal bastards produced by five ladies of the best families who granted James their favors.[19] Apparently, Lindsay was not guilty of overstatement in his *Answer to the King's Flyting*, and it is an intrepid scholar who would look for a prototype of Lady Sensualitie.

But these were royal failings which might have been overlooked or ignored—as Henry VIII's were—if the monarch's political sins of omission had been less discomfiting. At court, politics centered around a few powerful clerics and a group of young courtiers in sympathy with their ends. According to Sadler's more objective account, the overbalance of papal power could be explained by the scarcity of older men in Scotland, primarily because of the heavy loss of men at Flodden in 1513. As a result, the king was forced to appoint the clergy to the more responsible positions for they were "the men of wit and policy." The reformers were, for the most part, young men, and in matters of policy, their conservative elders generally swayed the king.[20] But whatever the objective reasons, the kirkman's sway was bitterly resented, and James could hardly have been unaware of it. The opinion of Protestant historians mirrors that of Alexander Seytoun, religious exile and formerly James V's confessor, who wrote his sovereign that the clergy had such "authoritie upoun they subjectes, that appearandly their war rather king, and thow the subject (quhilk injust regiment is of the selfe false, and contrair to holy Scripture and law of God)."[21] Worse yet, the prelates supported their proposals with pensioners, the courtiers closest to the king. Buchanan says that the courtiers condemned as heretical books sent by Henry VIII to James in 1535 after hardly looking at them,[22] and Pitscottie mutters that the same group supported the extension of heresy charges, knowing confiscated lands would be redistributed after heretics were condemned.[23]

One might dismiss much of this as the usual complaints of men out of power, if glimmers of the basis for such opinions did not come through contemporary sources. Knox tells us that James "lacked not flatteraris ynew; for many of his minzeonis war pensionaris to preastis; amongis whome, Oliver Synclar, yitt remaining ennemy to God, was the principale."[24] That gentleman, in addition to his position at court, was keeper of Tantallon, the castle confiscated from the earl of Angus after the latter's banishment in 1528. Along with his brother,

Sinclair was a member of the king's council; during summer's end in 1541, both brothers were staunch supporters of the clerical faction which successfully opposed Henry VIII's suggestion of a meeting between the two sovereigns at York, a plan supported by the Protestants who placed their hope for a reformed church on a sympathetic monarch.[25] That decision was the beginning of a more aggressive Scots policy, and the following year Oliver Sinclair briefly reached the pinnacle of power. But his triumph was short. The battle of Solway Moss took place on November 24, 1542. According to Hertford's subsequent intelligence, "the late roode made by the Scottes in the West Marches [Solway] was their kinges own acte by thadvice of the Cardynall, the Lorde Maxwell, Oliver Shenclere, and Mark Carre, much ageinst the willes and myndes of the rest of the counsaill, and lordes." [26] Hertford's spies corroborate the accounts of Knox, Pitscottie, and Buchanan who describe the nobles assembling their forces for the invasion of England, much against their will and minded "to hand all his secreit serwandis and consaluouris quhilk gaif him sic wickit consall contrarie the weillfair of his realme." [27] But James pushed his stubborn nobility too far when Sinclair, immediately before the battle began, produced the king's commission and banner and proclaimed himself commander of the army. The lords, insulted by this upstart's appointment, protested vehemently, and the army, in utter confusion, was overwhelmed by the smaller forces of their enemy and the treacherous ground of Solway swamp.[28] It was, for the English, a ridiculously easy victory with fat ransoms for captive gentry; for the Scots, it was the end of an era and the beginning of the painful ravages of the forties. For Oliver Sinclair, it was the finale of his brief power as upstart favorite; for James V, complete defeat, and, in December, death.

Scotland was plunged into confusion, and men once again traveled the public ways with weapons in their hand, ready for the ambush of enemy or thief.[29] The group which still thought of itself as vaguely "Lutherian" perhaps took some courage from the current chaos as Knox did later, interpreting the event: "When God had gevin unto that indurat Prince sufficient documentis, that his rebellioun against his blessed Evangell should not prosperouslie succeid, hie rases up against him warr, as that he did against obstinat Saull, in the which he miserablie perished." [30] Certainly Lindsay had said as much earlier, in his *Complaynt*, when he cautioned James that Idolators, like Jeroboam, were rooted out by God, and Rememberance's description of Scotland in *The Dreme* can be applied to 1542 as well as to 1528:

> So, I conclud that, throw the necligence
> Off our infatuate heidis Insolent,
> Is cause of all this realmes indigence,
> Quhilkis in Iustic hes nocht bene delygent,
> Bot to gude consall inobedient,
> Hauand small Ee vnto the comoun weill,
> Bot to thare singulare proffect euerilk deill.
>
> (ll. 904–10)

From this brief narration of James V's reign, it should be apparent that the first series of events in *Ane Satyre of the Thrie Estaitis* closely parallels the realities of Scots history as they were interpreted by contemporary writers. The king *was* introduced to sensuality by his courtiers and encouraged to continue that association; men in clerical garb *did* control the policies and acts of the state; and the king ultimately *did* feel the force of Divine Correction, the only emperor who could control kings. But King Humanitie, does not, like James V, die for his folly, nor is his story any more than one focus of the play's theme. Nor do the King's minions—Wantones, Placebo, and Sandie Solace—feel the weight of hatred and disdain poured out on James V's favorites. They are simply the silly agents who create a situation ripe for the entrance of Flatterie, Falset, and Dissait, the real villains of the piece.

Such difference can be explained by the events of 1542–52. With surprising swiftness, the dominant political forces converged on Edinburgh almost immediately after James's death. With the new queen only a few days old, David Cardinal Beaton, archbishop of Saint Andrews, was already forming the plans for a regency of four which would necessarily include himself. Such a measure would limit the power of James Hamilton, earl of Arran, Queen Mary's heir, and by tradition, the strongest claimant to the regency. By December 17, the news of James's death had already reached England, and Sir George Douglas had already correctly estimated the possibilities when he said, "therle of Arron was but a simple man. and thoder [heirs] were but foles, so that the strongest of the feelde were like to obteyne the coron." [31] At the beginning of January, the Douglases returned from their fourteen-year exile to become leaders of the "Assured Scots." The latter included the gentlemen prisoners of Solway Moss who, in exchange for their parole, promised to support English policies in the coming dispute. (As in many political maneuvers, their promises were as good as the English chance for success.) "The English lords," as they were scornfully called, found themselves faced with the powerful faction led by Cardinal Beaton, "the best Frenchman in Scotland,"[32] and their only real hope for control of the government lay with Arran, that "simple man." Viewed *ex post facto*, it was an impossible hope, but the reformers, supporting Douglas against the cardinal, were cheered by Arran's elevation, for he himself was a reader of the Testament and a supporter of the new ideas. Arran began auspiciously. In February, Cardinal Beaton was imprisoned on charges of treason, apparently to keep him out of the way for a time. A parliament was called where Arran officially became regent, and that most amazing act was passed on March 15 and proclaimed on the nineteenth: suddenly it was legal to read the Bible in English. Knox, with his usual awareness of character, describes the reaction:

> Then mycht have been sein the Byble lying almaist upoun everie gentilmanis table. The New Testament was borne about in many manis handes. We grant, that some (alace!) prophaned that blessed wourd; for some that, perchance, had never red ten sentenses in it, had it maist common in thare hand; thei wold chope thare familiares on the cheak with it, and say, "This hes lyne hyd under my bed-feitt these ten yearis." Otheris wold glorie, "O! how oft have I bein in danger from this booke: How secreatlie have I stollen fra my wyff at mydnycht to reid upoun it." And this was done of many to maik courte thairby; for all men esteamed the Governour to have bein the most fervent Protestant that was in Europa.[33]

But Arran the Governor was soon to give way to Arran the Puppet. At the same time, two of the three estates, clergy and commons, presented him with a three-point petition: he should restore Beaton to office unless treason could be proved against the cardinal; he should maintain the established religion; and he should appoint four nobles to care for the young queen. Shortly after, by some means, Beaton was mysteriously free again and back in his own castle of Saint Andrews. By the beginning of June, he was once again busy maintaining a large household where, according to English intelligence, he gave "greate fees, and such a hous was never holden in Scotlande undre a king."[34] Once again, the cardinal was the grand manipulator, and some saw his hand in the arrival of two important Scots who had been living in France. One was John Hamilton, Arran's bastard half

brother, abbot of Paisley, and still later Beaton's successor as the archbishop of Saint Andrews. By April 22, Arran had sent away the
"friers preachers, which he hath all this while defended" and, Sadler
tells us, the abbot of Paisley was "the only cause of the governour's
alteration; which abbot is all for France, and the cardinal's great
friend; and since his coming home, the governour hath been al-
together ruled by him." [35] The other arrival from France was the
earl of Lennox, Matthew Stuart, whose family held estates there.
Lennox himself played politics very badly, and in the end was the real
victim of Beaton's policy, but as next in line after Arran, he was a most
important pawn. [36] The bishop's faction quietly raised the old question
about the legality of the elder Hamilton's divorce before he married
Arran's mother; thus, James Hamilton, earl of Arran, was faced with
the possibility of being declared a legal bastard and forfeiting his
inheritance rights to Lennox.

Nevertheless, the cardinal's consolidation of power did not con-
geal until August. By July, the Douglas supporters saw the change
coming and began to desert to the better-paid and more powerful
French faction. By July 22, 1543, Beaton has amassed a huge force of
men and money, [37] and in early September, Arran capitulated. He was
shriven, given communion, blessed by Beaton's hand, and thereafter
docilely accepted his orders from the cardinal and Mary of Lorraine.
Later, in 1549, France rewarded him with the duchy of Châtellerault.
Bible reading was no longer sanctioned in Scotland, and the Scots
knew now their master was no longer "the poor man's king," but a
Roman priest. Persecution of heretics began again in November.

In less than a year, the reformers centered around Fife had first
seen their king punished by God with death and defeat and had
rejoiced at the new power of their faction with Arran's promotion.
But their reasons for joy were short-lived, and the turn of events even
more depressing in contrast to former expectations. Arran's
preachers were turned out, and their leaders were forced to leave the
court: Rothes, the laird of Grange, and perhaps Lindsay himself came
home to Fife defeated once more. [38] Arran and the cardinal made a
tour of Fife and Angus in November, a trip staged to further pul-
verize "by force and policy" the forces loyal to the Douglases. [39] The
court was controlled by "the best Frenchmen in Scotland": David
Beaton, who had been chief ambassador for James V's French mar-
riages and who held a benefice in France as well as those in Scotland;
John Hamilton, the abbot, illegitimate, educated in France, with rela-

tives in France, and newly arrived from France; David Panter, Hamilton's friend, who became ambassador to France in 1544 and, in 1547, bishop of Ross. Nor, should one forget, the Queen Mother's brother was a powerful cardinal of France.

Surely no one in Lindsay's audience in June, 1552, was insensitive to the innuendoes. The Vices have other characteristics besides the clerical garb they use as masquerade for irreligious motives. Dissait is illegitimate—the son of a whore; Scots prelates were often bastards of high birth. He is dressed as a gentleman (lines 676–77), and he casually utters his "Bon iour" (line 683). Flatterie himself arrives "new landit owt of france and stormested at the May," [40] and he urges his fellows to "keip graue countenance. / As wee war new cum out of France" (lines 723–24). It is these three who take over the government while King Humanite and his courtiers amuse themselves; it is they who accuse Veritie and Chastite of heresy; it is Flatterie, disguised as a Carmelite friar, who leads the inquisition of Johne the Common-Weill. Beaton, Hamilton, and their accessories, had done as much in their time, too.

But now it should be apparent that Lindsay, who turned his satire against the nobility in his *Complaynt*, chose new objects for the brunt of his wit in 1552. The courtiers are still there, but they are handled with relative disinterest except for their function as the initial perverters of the ruler. The real villains of the play are the clergy whose character provides the courtiers with the excuses for lechery, and the vices with ready entree to the court. The ire the reformers turned against their papist rulers and the French interest is a product of the decade after James V's death. Once more Scotland had seen a prince corrupted in Arran's rule, but this time the power of the prelates was greater. Lindsay's bitter picture of the clergy in *Ane Satyre of the Thrie Estaitis* reflects that awareness and that politico-religious strife.

The play also reflects another set of events. An unforeseen result of the power struggle in 1543 continued to plague Scotland until 1550. While the English faction tenuously held power in the spring and summer, Scotland and England had entered into a treaty whose major guarantee was the marriage of the young queen to Henry VIII's son. However, just a little more than a week after the treaties had been fomally completed, Arran joined the French faction. Henry, realizing the treaty was now worthless, began a new policy of harassment, and once again Scotland helplessly suffered English invasion. Winter delayed the first major attack, but in 1544 Hertford arrived with his ships and the English burnt Edinburgh, Holyrood, and Leith. In 1545, English attack was confined to the southern Lowlands. There the English reported burning seven monasteries—among them three of the most important in Scotland—and 240 villages. The following year was quiet, but in late 1547, the onslaught began again, and this time with greater force. In September, with their usual internal division, the Scots army lost the battle of Pinkie, and the English then proceeded to occupy and fortify Haddington, a town only eighteen miles from Edinburgh.[41] About the same time, "the auld enemy," sailing north into the Firth of Tay, burned Dundee and surrounding area in Angus. Early in 1548, they attempted a foray on the Fife peninsula, but were beaten off as they landed by the Fifeshire men.[42]

After the loss of Pinkie, the government entered into a new treaty with France, and Scotland was soon burdened with her French defenders. As with foreign allies everywhere, the people soon grew to resent them, and in 1548, a mob of Edinburgh citizens attacked some particularly offensive French soldiers; the Scots captain of the castle and several citizens were killed.[43] Caught between the French and the English, in many cases literally as well as politically, the people were enraged, and the peace that came in 1550, when France and England signed the Treaty of Boulogne, brought sorely needed calm to the desperate population.

In all these skirmishes which characterized the war, Fifeshire, of all the east-central coastline, perhaps suffered least. The one English invasion was repulsed, and the inevitable fire and pillage thus avoided; we hear of plague in Perth and Haddington, but there is no report of major epidemics in the Saint Andrews area. The Cupar citizens, hearing of neighboring disasters, must have felt anxiously fortunate. But another sort of storm was reserved for them. In February, 1546, they witnessed at Saint Andrews the trial and burning of George Wishart, the man who was to become the symbol of Scots religious reform. Three months later, on May 29, they heard the astounding news that Cardinal Beaton, the arch-villain in the reformers' struggle, had been murdered by their neighbors. The long seige of Saint Andrews began. It lasted for over a year, while the government vainly tried to break the rebels' hold on the well-fortified castle. Finally, in July, the always-obliging French sent sea aid; the castle's sea walls were bombarded and destroyed; the "Castilians," as the rebels were called by that time, were taken on board the ships.

Both the assassins and some of the leading reformers who had joined them in Saint Andrews after the murder were taken to France—some to imprisonment, some to a sentence as galley slaves for France. Among the former was Henry Balnaves, self-made man, sometime ambassador to England, and a leader of the reformers at court. It was he who had spoken the faction's arguments in 1543 for the parliamentary act permitting Scots to read the Bible. Among those sentenced to hard labor in the ships was John Knox, already a man in his thirties, an ordained priest who, during the previous spring, had just discovered his calling to preach the reformed doctrine.[44] The Fifeshire protestants had cause to weep when they saw their friends and leaders taken into the French captivity.[45]

But it was Lothian, the area across the firth from Fife, which bore the extreme suffering of the war. By November, 1549, five months before peace finally came, the people's lot was extreme. It is ironic, perhaps, from our reformer's viewpoint, that Mary of Lorraine, the brilliant dowager queen, gives us a most explicit description of that suffering:

> Et fot, à ce propos, que je vous die que, sy le Roy ne donne queque ordre à' sa quevalerye qu'yl a pardesa, notre peis ne saroit sueporte les mos quy font. Car y vous fot antandre que notre peisant n'a rien à' luy et ne demeure seu le tere que sin ou sis ans, et ce pendant les povre jans gagne se quy peulve pour vivre. Sy sont otes, y fot quy belle le fermes à leur metres de fourmant te d'orge; de quoy y ne leur reste que l'avoine de quoy vive. On le met dehors de leur meson; ung n'a james poie ung liart de noriteure de chevas. Y breule le boys quy se trouve dedans la meson, comme bans table et telle chose. Se povre endroit de pais a souteneu la guerre euit ans, et tous le jours breule des anemis. Je vous proumes que s'e chose ynseuportable; y se mete au dessepoir et s'an teue queque fois.[46]

The pauper's identity as a poor man from Tranent in Lothian perhaps had other nuances of meaning for the Cupar audience. For the last few years, the poor of Lothian had been poor indeed, and a man who had cows to be taken by parish priests must have had an extremely hardhearted vicar.

Faced with the ultimate disasters in human life, the Scots, like all men, searched for a reason, an explanation. Once again the reformers turned to their jealously guarded Bible and found, in the Old Testament wars and captivities, their answer. A just God must chastise his people. Until all Scotsmen lifted their erring nation out of Romish idolatry, the congregation, the enlightened protestants, must bear God's discipline visited on the sins of the entire people. It was the principle of divine correction, and that principle is embodied, in Lindsay's play, as Correctioun, the reformer and the deliverer of the nation who takes vengance "sum tyme with swerd and pestilence, / With derth and povertie" (lines 2266–67). Again and again, Knox, Pitscottie, Buchanan point out the evidence for this view in their accounts of 1544–50. Knox summarizes the hard winter and spring of 1547–48, when the English were firmly entrenched: "Thus did God plague in everie quarter; butt men war blynd, and wold nott, nor could nott, considder the cause." [47] Pitscottie interprets the defeat at Pinkie as evidence that the English "war bot instrumentis of god in that cace to punische thame witht weir that wald nocht grant to peace and refussit so money fair offaris to thair distructioun." [48] Robert Burrant, justifying the murder of Cardinal Beaton, cites the fate of biblical tyrants and interprets Beaton's death: "the secrete judgements of God . . . hath . . . bene nowe declared by the moste wretched slaughter of thys member of Antichriste." [49] So the Scots saw the hand of God in their own time and found some hope and comfort even in the divine wrath visited on Scotland.

At Cupar in Whitsuntide 1552, in a time of peace only two years old, the people must have remembered the recent past as they watched Lindsay's holiday play. King Correctioun was not a stranger to them, and only they, perhaps, could fully appreciate the bitterness of the Fool's lines, "Quhat cummer have ӡe had in Scotland / Be our auld enemies of Ingland?" (lines 4564–65).

Whatever else it may have been, the period between 1542 and 1552 must have seen definite growth in the ranks of the reformers who, by 1560, were strong enough to seize the government and begin the period of Protestant dominance which ultimately resulted in a Scots form, Presbyterianism. It is difficult to estimate the Protestants' numbers before 1560. Certainly their political defeat in 1542 implies that the group was small and held little real power, but the movement had only really begun with the arrival of Patrick Hamilton who, in 1528, became the first "Lutherian" preacher and martyr. It is equally difficult to estimate the impact of the heresy trials which punctuated the years between 1528 and 1552. For the Scots, there is no collection of tales comparable to those of the English in Foxe's *Acts and Monuments*, and we must depend primarily on those few accounts which survive in Foxe and in Knox. But this material usually reveals the stories only of those condemned to death, although general statements tell us many people recanted or escaped into exile. If we do not know the number who escaped death, we do know of sixteen people who were executed for heresy in that twenty-four year period: Hamilton in 1528; Gourlay and Stratton in 1534; Thomas Forret and four others in 1539; Kennedy and Russell later in 1539; four men and a woman in Perth in 1544; and Adam Wallace in 1550. All were publicly burned, except the woman who was drowned. One man, Sir John Borthwick, was burned in effigy in 1540 after he had escaped into exile.[50]

The facts themselves are rather bare, and, in our age of mass executions, not particularly impressive in their number. But until one has read the few remaining accounts of the heresy trials, imagined the smell of burning flesh and the reactions of the reformers to the spectacles, it is hardly possible to appreciate the bitterness implicit in the two heresy indictments in *Ane Satyre*. Lindsay's representation includes no burnings, but the threat is there, and the audience at Cupar knew the reality of that threat from their own experience. More than that, the trial accounts convey the character of those sixteen human beings who obstinately and faithfully died for their beliefs, and they remind us, living as we are in a secular age, of the literal and crucial importance of questions of faith and religious practice to men who knew that life was only preparation for immortality. Like reformers in all ages, their faith, at the beginning, primarily consisted of a denial of the status quo with a few passionately held convictions which were expanded and developed as the movement progressed. For these criticisms, they suffered.

But it is the quality of the heresy trials which interest us as the background for the *Thrie Estaitis*. While the play itself contains only a few definite identifications with events, the general tone is so close to contemporary reports that the area of reference is unmistakable. In general, Lindsay selected from actual events two types who generally represent the range of those accused of heresy. The first is Veritie, the learned person whose mission is teaching and preaching "Christ and his law," the simple definition of the *Veritie*.[51] Such a person was an educated teacher of the people and was frequently a priest who had severed his connection with the established church only by adopting reforming opinions. At her first appearance, Veritie utters the all-too-familiar plea for a just judge, a plea that the "heretics" sounded again and again. Jeronimus Russell, a Cordelier friar burned at Glasgow in 1539, was reputed to have said at his trial: "This is your houre and the power of darknes: now sytt ye as judgeis; and we stand wrongfullie accused, and more wrongfullie to be condempned; but the day shall come, when our innocency shall appear, and that ye shall see your awin blyndness, to your everlesting confusioun. Go fordward, and fulfill the measur of your iniquitie." [52] At his trial at Saint Andrews in 1546, George Wishart put forth a similar plea, and when his accusers asked if Cardinal Beaton were not an adequate judge, Wishart responded: "I refuse not my Lorde Cardinall, but I desire the worde of god to be my judge, and the temporal estate. w[ith] some of your Lordeshippes myne auditours, because I am here my Lord Gouernours [Arran's] prisoner." [53] In Edinburgh, the cry was raised again in 1550 by a simple man, Adam Wallace:

> The Bischoppes can be no judges to me; for thei ar oppen ennemyes to me and to the doctrin that I professe. And as for my Lord Duck, [Arran] I can not tell yf he hes the knowledge that should be in him that should judge and decerne betuix lyes and the trewth, the inventionis of men and the trew wirschipping of God. I desyre Goddis word . . . to be judge betuix the Bischoppes and me, and I am content that ye all hear, and yf by this book, I salbe convict to have tawght, spokin, or done, in materis of religioun, any thing that repugnes to Goddis will, I refuise not to dye; but yf I can nott be convict, (as I am assured by Goddis woord I shall nott,) then I in Goddis name desyre your assistance, that malicious men execut not upoun me injust tyranny.[54]

All these accounts are not, of course, trial transcripts, and we will never be sure how much is the writer's invention, how much the word of the man accused. But their accuracy or inaccuracy is not a question here. Whatever the martyrs really said, the lack of a just judge is associated with their trials, and it is thus fitting for Veritie to echo their pleas in her first speech:

> *Diligite Iustitiam qui iudicastis terram.*
>
> Luif Iustic ȝe quha hes ane Iudges cure
> In earth, and dreid the awfull Iudgement
> Of him that sall cum iudge baith rich and pure,
> Rycht terribilly with bludy wound[i]s rent.
> That dreidfull day into ȝour harts imprent:
> Belevand weill how and quhat maner ȝe

Vse Iustice heir til vthers, thair at lenth
That day but doubt sa sall ʒe iudgit be.
Wo than and duill be to ʒow Princes all,
Sufferand the pure anes for till be opprest
In everlasting burnand fyre ʒe sall
With Lucifer richt dulfullie be drest.

(Ll. 1026–38)

She continues, in traditional fashion, to contrast the just and the unjust judge, applying her terms to the Scots bishops, but the cue is
already there. From the moment of her first appearance, Veritie is
identified as the Protestant's truth, "Christ and his law," warning that
hell-fire awaits the judge who sends "the pure anes" to the stake.

For further analysis, we will concentrate on George Wishart's trial.
The reasons are several. Wishart's trial and execution was the single
most important event in the early Scottish movement. Working
primarily in the area around the Firth of Forth, Wishart was the most
important minister to emerge before Knox became undisputed
leader, and he was thus widely known. His reputation became inter-
national when his execution was followed by the assassination of Cardinal Beaton and the rebellion of a small group of reformers who
held the prelate's castle of Saint Andrews against the Governor's seige
from May 29, 1546, until July, 1547. In true sixteenth-century fashion, a book was published with a preface by Robert Burrant defend-
ing the godliness of the assassination. It contained the account of
Wishart's trial and death (which was subsequently used by Foxe,
Knox, and Pitscottie) and Lindsay's *The Tragedie of the Late Cardinal
Beaton* which was written in January, 1547.[55] Of all the heresy accounts, that of George Wishart is the most trustworthy. It was written
soon enough after the event to imply a fresh memory; it is an "official" account to the world, and while it must certainly be characterized
as biased, it must just as certainly convey the picture the reformers
wished to present. Most important to us, the event happened at Saint
Andrews, only a few miles from Cupar; Lindsay himself associated
with the "Castillians" during their defense of the castle,[56] and he
himself wrote the official account of Beaton's murder which appeared
in the same book with the standard account of Wishart's fate. For
these reasons, George Wishart's trial is a sound choice as a general
parallel to Veritie's accusation.

This is not to say that the article is a source for the play. It is useful
for another reason: the protestant view of their persecutors and the

image of the ideal martyr are revealed in the tract, and we shall see that these attitudes underlie the portrayal of Veritie and her antagonists. The contrast between accusers and accused was summarized by Foxe, as he introduced the tract in his book:

> Ponder . . . the furious rage and tragical cruelness of the malignant church, in persecuting of this blessed man of God; and, on the contrary, his humble, patient, and most godly answers made to them suddenly without all fear, not having respect to their glorious menacings and boisteous threats, but charitably and without stop of tongue answering.[57]

Lindsay portrays the "malignant" motives of the accusers in a short scene preceding their confrontation of Veritie, the potential martyr. Those motives center on simple and straightforward self interest. Flatterie speaks for his faction: "Be scho ressauit but doubt wee ar bot schent: / Let hir nocht ludge thairfoir into this Land" (lines 1093–94). Spiritualitie repeats the theme, "Be scho ressauit then wee will be deprysit" (line 1103), and the Abbot recommends a heresy trial saying, "For with the King gif Veritie be knawin, / Of our griet gloir wee will degradit be, / And all our secreits to the commouns schawin" (lines 1110–12). According to the reformers' account, the motive of the clerics at Wishart's trial was essentially the same: "Than all the whole congregation of the prelates wyth their complices, sayed these wordes. And if we give him licence to preache, he is so craftie, and in the holy scripture so exercised, that he wyll persuade the people to his opinion, and rayse them agaynste us." [58] From the reformers' point of view, the prelates persecute, not from a concern for heresy or religious falsehood, but from fear for the security of power, their hold over the people. It is not a battle between opposing ideas, but a battle between spiritual right and worldly wrong.

Parsone and Flatterie's brief dialogue with Veritie exemplifies the contrast between the opposing sides. Their first words to her are an explicit challenge and threat:

> To preich or teich quha gaif to ȝow command,
> To counsall Kingis how gat ȝe commissions?
> I dreid without ȝe get ane remissioun,
> And syn renunce ȝour new opiniones,
> The sprituall stait sall put ȝow to perditioun,
> And in the fyre will burne ȝoe flesche and bones.
>
> (Ll. 1130–35)

Flatterie follows this by calling her "harlot" and accusing her of heresy for possession of an English Bible. Such words convey the same rough power and disdain attributed to Wishart's accusers who fling out: "Thou hereticke, runnagate, traytor, and thiefe. It was not lawful for the to preache. Thow haste taken the power at thyne owne hande, without any authoritie of the churche, we forthynke that thou haste bene a preacher to longe." [59]

In contrast, both the fictional character and the actual man respond to their accuser with the firm gentleness of the ideal Christian, and at the end of their inquisition offer a sweet prayer unto the Lord for the benefit of all true believers in the veritie. Wishart's begins:

> O Immortall god, howe long shalt thou suffre the wodnesse and greate crudelitie of the ungodlie, to exercise their fury upon the seruantes whiche do farther thy word in this world seeyinge they desyre to be contrarie. . . . Lord we knowe suerly that thy trewe seruauntes must needes suffre for thy names sake persecutioun, affliction, and troubles in thys present lyfe. . . . But yet we desyre the hertely, that thou conserue, defende, and helpe thay congregation. . . . And geve thame thy grace to heare thy worde, and to be thy trewe seruauntes in thys present life. [60]

Veritie speaks on the same theme:

> For our christs saik I am richt weill content
> To suffer all thing that sall pleis his grace;
> . . . .
> Get vp, thow sleipis all to lang, O Lord,
> And mak sum ressonabill reformatioun
> O them that dois tramp doun thy gracious word,
> And hes ane deidlie indignatioun
> At them quha makes maist trew narratioun:
> Suffer me not Lord, mair to be molest,
> Gude Lord, I mak the supplicatioun,
> With thy vnfreinds let me nocht be supprest.
> (Ll. 1156–57, 1160–67)

In contrast to the description of Wishart's trial and execution, Lindsay's presentation of Veritie's similar situation is brief and condensed. The effect of the heresy accusation and arrest in the play rests on the knowledge of comparable events, known to the Cupar citizens. That audience would know such arrests were immediately followed with death by fire, and their fear for Veritie would be based on experience. The portrayal of the characters involved rests on attitudes comparable to those in the tract published in 1548: the persecutors are evil and self-seeking; the persecuted are innocent and pure. Lindsay's scene is brief, but, in its brevity, it conveys the condition and hopes of his own religious minority: a plea for justice and recognition of the destructive elements in control of Scots society.

It does not, however, tell the whole story, and Lindsay balances this first account with a second accusation later in the play. Here the exemplar is Johne the Common-Weill, the stubborn, honest, uneducated man who freely speaks his mind against the injustices of the church only to find himself caught in a senseless charge of heresy. As the theme of the clergy's lust for power runs through their attack of Veritie, so Johne's case exemplifies a common theme. It is first enunciated by Johne himself when he is invited to elaborate on his charges, "Na, sir, I dar nocht speik ane word. / To plaint on Preistis it is na bourd" (lines 2740–41). The Parsone repeats the refrain, "To speik of Preists be sure it is na bourds: / Thay will burne men now for rakless words" (lines 2773–74), and Spiritualitie himself repeats the warning a few lines later, "I let ʒow wit my Lords it is na bourds. / Of Prelats for till speik sic wantoun words" (lines 2781–82). The rhyme is not without objective reference, for Knox himself makes the same charge: "But so fearfull it was then to speak any thing against preastis, that the least word spokin against thame, yea albeit it was spokin in a manes sleip, was judged heresye." [61] Johne, however, heartened by his sympathetic superiors, proceeds to charge monks and friars with idleness and sloth, parish priests with excessive and ruinous exactions of death dues, and the clergy in general with sexual lust and avarice. These are serious charges, but they are charges heard again and again throughout the reformers' literature. Surely the audience must have remembered instances when simple men had uttered similar complaints. Thomas Forret (executed, 1539), the vicar of Dollar, was reprimanded by his superior for refusing to collect the "corse present," the fee for burial, from his parishioners, but he was a priest who taught the reformers' doctrine. They might rather have remembered the Perth martyrs of 1543 who were commoners. Robert Lamb was tried and burned after he interrupted a friar's sermon, accused him "in open audience of erroneous doctrine, and adjured him, in God's name, to utter the truth." James Hunter, "flesher by occupation," was accused "because he often used ... suspected company." James

Ravelson, a carpenter, and William Anderson were accused of mockery for what we should consider rather improper but amusing practical jokes.[62] Or, remembering back into the thirties, they might have thought of David Stratton, a gentleman, who was burned after he had referred contemptuously to his own excommunication. He was cursed by the church for refusing to pay his tithes and for telling his fisherman to throw every tenth fish they caught back into the sea, saying "if thei wald haif teynd of that which his servandis wane in the sea, it war but reassoun, that thei should come and receave it whare hie gatt the stock." [63]

But rough Scots humor was not always repaid by fire. When Johne flings out his charge that the prelates "lyke rams rudlie in thair rage, / Vnpysalt rinnis amang the sillie ʒowis, / Sa lang as kynde of nature in them growis" (lines 2764–66), some in the audience may have remembered the story of Sandie Furrour who came home from the wars after seven years as a prisoner in England only to discover that his wife and her lover, a priest, had wasted his money. The Scots Ulysses wasted no time in trumpeting his disgust with priests and "priest's whores" and soon found himself at Saint Andrews facing the assembled bishops of the realm on a heresy charge. Answering the charges with charges of his own, Furrour culminated his mocking, indignant replies by addressing the assembled bishops: "Becaus I complayne of such injuries, I am hear summoned, and accused, as one that is worthy to be brunt. For Goddis saik, (said he), wil ye taick wyeffis of your awin, that I and utheris, whose wyiffis ye have abused, may be revenged upon yow." The old bishop of Aberdeen, like the Parsone in the *Thrie Estaitis* (lines 2767–69), responded with shock, "Carll, thow shalt not know my wyff," to which the intrepid Sandie answered, "My Lord, ye ar too old; bot, with the grace of God, I shall drynk with your dochtter or I departe." Everyone, it seems, knew the bishop had a married daughter who lived in Saint Andrews. Sandie Furrour was released, but not before he had forced the clergy present at his trial to give him money "to begyn my pack agane, which a preast and my wyif, a preastis hoore, hes spentt." [64] Johne the Common-Weill does not use the same words as Sandie Furrour, but his tone of honest insolence is the same when he offers to prove his charge on the parson's pallet. And, one would think, Temporalitie replies, with a grin, to Spiritualitie's complaint: "Quhy my Lord, sayis he ocht bot verity? / ʒe can nocht stop ane pure man for till pleinʒe. / Gif he hes faltit summond him to your Seinʒe" (lines 2748–86). The audience knew of at least one man who had made fools of the bishops at their seinȝe, and Spiritualitie, aware of dangerous ground, quickly shifts the debate to another topic.

One other element in Johne's debate comes close to a more contemporary parallel, and that is his recitation of the Creed when he faces the literal accusation of heresy. First of all, in June, 1552, it was still a little daring for Johne to recite the Credo in English and in public. True, the church's Provincial Council in January, 1552, had authorized the publication of a catechism, but the book was not published until the following August, and even that liberal document implies some hedging on the sensitive question of prayers in the vernacular. Only the Pater Noster appears in English at the beginning of the section where its explanation begins. The other prayers, the Ave and the Credo, are translated, each line separately, after the Latin line is given, with an exposition on each line, in the short sermons which form two chapters of the catechism.[65] Just as important, the incomplete form of the Creed (without the section beginning, "I believe in the holy Catholic church . . .") which Johne recites in English is essentially the same that Adam Wallace recited at his heresy trial in 1550. Moreover, Wallace prefaced his recitation with the observation, "I have not much Latin," which appears to suggest he knew the priests would not relish his use of English.[66] With the memory of Wallace's trial and the recent controversy on prayers in the vernacular, [67] Johne the Common-Weill's Creed is a daring representation indeed, and the reformers in the Cupar audience must have felt an unfamiliar sense of public vindication when Correctioun judges Johne "ane gude Christian man" (line 3030). Johne, the common man, unlike his martyred counterparts, escapes the fire.

In contrast to the sympathetic treatment of the reformers, the theme of the clergy's ignorance, so cleverly lampooned by the reference to the Pater Noster controversy in the play's final lines, is embellished by comparable parodies of clerical attitudes. Certainly the Pardoner incorporates some of the reformers' favorite mockeries. He enters, shortly after the play's intermission with his bag of tricks, bemoaning the slack season that has come over his business now that people are reading the New Testament. He seems confused about the book's character and roundly curses all those who encourage its dispersion:

> Duill fell the braine that hes it wrocht
> Sa fall them that the Buik hame brocht:

> Als I pray to the Rude
> That Martin Luther that fals loun
> Black Bullinger and Melancthoun,
>   Had bene smorde in their cude.
> Be him that buir the crowne of thorne,
> I wald Sanct Paull had neuer bene borne
>   And als I wald his buiks
> War never red into the kirk.

(Ll. 2068–77)

The Pardoner's distress apparently mimics the attiude of some of the clergy, for Buchanan tells us, "such was the general ignorance, that many of the priests, offended at the term *New*, contended that it was a book lately written by Martin Luther, and demanded the *Old Testament*." [68] Similarly, the mock divorce of Sowtar and his wife may be taken seriously as well as in jest, for in 1550, on the same day at the same Edinburgh court where Adam Wallace was tried for heresy, a priest named John Ker was accused and convicted of falsely divorcing a man and wife, on his own authority. His sentence was banishment and loss of his benefices; Wallace's sentence was death, and the Cupar audience may have seen the same irony in the play when Veritie is imprisioned and a friar casually devises a divorce.[69]

But it is Wilkin, the Pardoner's boy, who strikes a direct hit when he tells his master that "Sum syais ʒe are ane verie loun: / Sum sayis, *Legatus natus*" (lines 2193–94). The only man who possessed that title in Scotland was the archbishop of Saint Andrews, and the apparently casual insertion of the title gives added point to the lines that follow:

> Bot keip ʒow fra subiectioun,
> Of the curst King Correctioun:
> . . . .
> For be ye with him fangit,
>   But doubt ʒe will be hangit.

(Ll. 2193–94, 2200, 2203)

One *legatus natus*, Cardinal Beaton, had already been "corrected" by assassination; his successor, John Hamilton, had since continued Beaton's policies. The audience must have appreciated the ironically casual application of the archbishop's title to the rascal Pardoner who lies and cheats with zest.

The events preceding Johne the Common-Weill's heresy trial make similar use of popular knowledge and are linked to the

Pardoner's scene by a variation of the Pardoner's lines, "Sum sayis by him that woare the croun of thorne, / It had been gude that Paull had neir bene borne" (lines 2915–16, cf. 2076–77). Again, the topic is the Bible, and Spiritualitie echoes the bishop of Dunkeld in his reply. Some time before Thomas Forret, vicar of Dollar, was burned for heresy, the bishop of Dunkeld, his superior, reproved him for his liberal practices as a parish priest. When the conversation turned to the use of the Bible in sermons, Foxe reports, the bishop said, "I thank God that I never knew what the Old and New Testament was," and, Foxe adds, "of these words rose a proverb which is common in Scotland, Ye are like the Bishop of Dunkeldene, that knew neither new nor old law." [70] The same bishop was instrumental in Forret's arrest for heresy and was one of those officially present at the vicar's trial in 1539. It is with a certain appropriateness, then, that Spiritualitie joins the bishop's sentiment with an oath by Judas:

> Na sir, be him that our Lord Jesus sauld
> I red never the New testament nor auld:
> Nor ever thinks to do sir be the Rude.
> I heir freiris say that reiding dois na gude
>
> (Ll. 2919–22)

Joining the Pardoner and Spiritualitie together, Lindsay used the commonplace taunts of the reformers to expose his clerics' ignorance. We shall never know how much parody of personalities may have appeared in the production of the play. Actors could easily have adapted the mannerisms of living people to their roles, and one would think they would have mimicked the powerful as much as they safely could. But that sort of record is irreparably lost, and the Scots manuscript sources that may provide clues to personal characteristics are generally so unexplored that one would have to write a social history of the period before completing a literary analysis of the play which *might* include personal identifications. At least in general, the history of the Scots reformers is essential for understanding *Ane Satyre of the Thrie Estaitis*, both in terms of general tone and specific event. What further research may or may not reveal is anyone's guess.

What I have been investigating here may be simply described. I have asked what assumptions Lindsay might have made about the history of his own time and his audience's knowledge of it. We are fortunate enough to find the struggle narrated by members of

Lindsay's faction, some of whom themselves knew the dramatist. Studying a time and place where materials are relatively limited, we have nevertheless been able to see how closely the play generally reflects the reformers' attitudes and experiences. For our purposes, the lack of objectivity in the sources is a virtue, for if we are to understand the play, we must acquire the reformers' reactions. Curiously enough, then, this has been a study in search of subjectivity. My description of events is not "true" in the objective sense; it is merely the truth as the reformers tell it and as *Ane Satyre of the Thrie Estaitis* reflects it.

From the material presented in this chapter, the importance of contemporary Scots history should be self-evident. We cannot expect to be very much interested in King Humanitie's turn to sensuality unless we remember James V and the earl of Arran and see that the king's action in the play is a generalization rising out of Scots political experience. We can scarcely appreciate the courtiers without the memory of men like Oliver Sinclair, nor the Vices without an awareness of Cardinal Beaton and Archbishop Hamilton. Similarly, King Correctioun is no more than a mechanical plot device except when we know, as the Scots at Cupar knew, that he represents the horror of war, famine, plague, and murder as those people in 1552 only too well remembered them. Against such a background, Lindsay did not need to fill in details which he could assume his audience would know and recognize.

More important, without some awareness of the reformers' passionate response to their persecution and passionate defense of their religious—and political—position, no literary critic can imagine the audience's response to the play. Without this involvement, we cannot fully understand Lindsay's presentation of Veritie, Johne the Common-Weill, and the various clerics grouped around them, nor can we expect to feel the implicit threat of death in the heresy accusations which seem so simple to our twentieth-century minds.

Once we have seen the play in the context of events from 1526 to 1552, we can begin to understand its nature and structure. Like Marlowe's *Edward II*, the *Thrie Estaitis* incorporates a long span of history but, unlike Marlowe, Lindsay did not face the pitfalls of realistic representation. Yet, through a different mode of representation (which we shall examine in later chapters), Lindsay no less than Marlowe dramatizes his nation's history. Since he does, we must imaginatively re-create the times and his characters as images, not of opposing forces described in a history book, but of living men like ourselves who bitterly fought each other on an issue of central importance to all of them. *Ane Satyre of the Thrie Estaitis* is no mere "morality" play, for it does not merely moralize. As in all drama, this morality play "holds the mirror up to nature" to show men their own experience. If we do not understand that experience or the terms in which it is stated, the artist is not to blame.

NOTES

1. *Satire* is used loosely here, since it is not a main focus of this study. For more intensive discussion of the term, see A. R. Heiserman's *Skelton and Satire* (Chicago: University of Chicago Press, 1962), and John D. Peter's *Complaint and Satire in Early English Literature* (Oxford: Clarendon Press, 1956). Lindsay's use of the word in his title seems to reflect a view of drama which divides it into three genres: tragedy, comedy, and satire. See C. A. Mayer's " 'Satyre' as a Dramatic Genre," *Bibliotheque d'Humanisme et Renaissance* 13 (1951): 327–33; D. J. Shaw, "More about the 'Dramatic Satyre,' " *BHR* 30 (1968): 301–25; H.-R. Jauss, "Literature médiévale et théorie des genres," *Poetique* 1 (1970): 79–101, which includes a bibliography.

2. *The Bannatyne Manuscript*, 3:101.

3. *Ibid.*, p. 30.

4. *The State Papers and Letters of Sir Ralph Sadler*, ed. Arthur Clifford, 2 vols. (Edinburgh: Archibald Constable and Co., 1809), 1:19, 22, 44 (hereafter cited as Sadler, *Papers*).

5. Privy Council to Suffolk, 28 Dec. 1543. *The Hamilton Papers*, ed., Joseph Bain, vol. 2 (Edinburgh: H. M. General Register House, 1890), p. 242. wood and Sons, 1899), l:xxxv, cxv.

6. Robert Lindesay of Pitscottie, *The Historie and Chronicles of Scotland*, ed., A. J. G. MacKay, 2 vols., Scottish Text Society (Edinburgh: William Blackwood and Sons, 1899), 1:xxv, cxv.

7. *Ibid.*, pp. cix, cxxi.

8. *The Works of John Knox*, ed. David Laing, 6 vols. (Edinburgh: The Bannatyne Club, 1846–64), 1:186 (hereafter cited as Knox, *Works*). Unless otherwise noted, this is the edition to which I refer in the text.

9. Although published much later, Knox's history was begun in 1560, continued and revised in 1566. This was roughly the same time when Foxe was working on his *Acts and Monuments* which was published in its Latin edition in 1559, later revised extensively and published in a second edition in 1570. Both Knox and Foxe used the book on George Wishart's trial which contains Lindsay's *Tragedie of the Late Cardinal Beaton*. The latter was printed by John Daye about 1548. Daye also published *Acts and Monuments* where the

Wishart account was reprinted in 1563; in 1570, Fox labeled the Wishart text "ex histor. impressa" (see p. 1109), an acknowledgement of his source. I also make ancillary use of George Buchanan's history which was completed in 1579, at the end of his life. He had been at the court of James V during the 1530s, but spent the forties and fifties abroad, not returning to Scotland until the early 1560s. Buchanan was a favorite student of John Major, one of Pitscottie's sources. The date for Pitscottie's history is not clear, nor has his work been studied adequately. We must still rely on the text edited by A. J. G. MacKay in 1899. MacKay also wrote the entry on Pitscottie for the *Dictionary of National Biography*; it, too, provides confusing dates. Gordon Donaldson's *Scotland: James V to James VIII* (Edinburgh: Oliver and Boyd, 1965), provides an authoritative and scholarly account of the period discussed here. In "James V and the Scottish Church, 1528–1542," J. Wilson Ferguson works from the printed sources used in this chapter. (See *Action and Conviction in Early Modern Europe*, ed. Theodore K. Rabb and Jerrold Siegel [Princeton: Princeton University Press, 1969].)

10. See W. Croft Dickinson's introduction to his modernized text of Knox's *History of the Reformation in Scotland*, 2 vols. (London: Thomas Nelson and Sons, 1949), p. lxxxi. The standard biography of Knox is Jasper Ridley's *John Knox* (Oxford: Oxford University Press, 1968).

11. It is possible to argue for a more limited time span, but such a limitation would cut the range of possible associations, and the reference of the play itself does not seem to permit limitation to only one set of historical figures or circumstances.

12. All quotations from the play are taken from the 1602 reprint in Douglas Hamer's edition of *The Works of Sir David Lindsay*. Quotations from other Lindsay works are from the appropriate texts in vol. 1.

13. In matters of dating, I follow William Croft Dickinson's *Scotland from the Earliest Time to 1603* (London: Thomas Nelson, 1961).

14. Hamer, ed., *Works*, 3:47.

15. See, for example, Sir William Eure's letter, Hamer, ed., *Works*, 2:2–6; Henry Charteris's preface to his 1568 edition of Lindsay's works, reprinted in Hamer, ed., *Works*, 1:398; and David Calderwood, *History of the Kirk of Scotland*, ed. Thomas Thomson, vol. 1 (Edinburgh: The Woodrow Society, 1842), 146–47. But cf. Gordon Donaldson, *Scotland: James V to James VII*, pp. 43–62, especially 61–62. There, the judgment of James V is more severe.

16. Pitscottie, *History and Chronicles of Scotland*, 1:408–9.

17. Knox, *Works*, 1:93; George Buchanan, *Rerum Scoticarum Historia*, trans. J. Aikman, 6 vols. (Glasgow: Blackie and Son, 1856), bk. 14, pars. lvi, lxii; Sadler, *Papers*, 1:47; *Hamilton Papers*, 1:74.

18. *Letters of James V*, ed. Denys Hay (Edinburgh: Her Majesty's Stationery Office, 1954), pp. 279–426 and index entries, p. 466. See also A. R. Macewen, *A History of the Church in Scotland*, 2 vols. (London: Hodder and Stoughton, 1913, 1918), 2:441.

19. The children were James (primus), James (secundus)—later Regent Moray—John, Robert, all born between 1529 and 1533, and a daughter called Jane, Janet, or Jean. The ladies were Elizabeth Carmichael, Elizabeth Beaton, Margaret Erskine, Euphemia Elphinstone, and a daughter of David Lindsay, eighth earl of Crawford. See the index and references in W. C. Dickinson's edition of Knox.

20. Sadler, *Papers*, 1:47.

21. Knox, *Works*, 1:49.

22. Buchanan, *Rerum Scoticarum Historia*, bk. 14, par. 1.

23. Pitscottie, *History and Chronicles of Scotland*, 1:404.

24. Knox, *Works*, 1:67.

25. Sir Thomas Wharton to the Privy Council, 2 Sept. [1541]. *Hamilton Papers*, 1:99.

26. Hertford to the Privy Council, 1 Dec. 1542. *Hamilton Papers*, 1:314. Concerning Oliver Sinclair, see also the following letters in the *Hamilton Papers*, vol. 1: Hertford to Henry VII, 27 Nov. 1542, Appendix, p. xc; Saville and Wentworth to Privy Council, 16 Dec. 1542, p. 335; George Douglas to Lisle, 16 Dec. [1542], p. 338; Henry VIII's instructions, Jan. 1542/43, pp. 367, 368; Lisle to Henry VIII, 21 Jan. 1542/43, p. 390; Suffolk and Tunstall to Privy Council, 11 June 1543, p. 539; Suffolk to Privy Council, 11 June 1543, p. 540. He is also mentioned in the *Diurnal of Occurents*, ed. Thomas Thomson, p. 37. The entry is dated 20 Jan. 1544/45.

27. Pitscottie, *History and Chronicles of Scotland*, 1:402.

28. Knox, *Works*, 1:88; Pitscottie, *History and Chronicles of Scotland*, 1:402; Buchanan, *Rerum Scoticarum Historia*, bk. 14, par. lxi.

29. See Lisle to Privy Council, 21 Dec. 1542, *Hamilton Papers*, 1:344–45; Lisle to Henry VIII, 5 Jan. 1542/43, ibid., p. 359.

30. Knox, *Works*, 1:76.

31. Lisle and Tunstall to Henry VII, *Hamilton Papers*, 1:337.

32. Sadler, *Papers*, 1:93.

33. Knox, *Works*, 1:100–101.

34. Parr to Suffolk, 8 June 1543, *Hamilton Papers*, 1:537.

35. George Douglas's comments to Sadler, in Sadler, *Papers*, 1:158, 160.

36. For a clear estimate of Lennox's abilities, see *Two Missions of Jacques de la Brosse*, ed. Gladys Dickinson, Scottish History Society ser. 3, vol. 36 (Edinburgh: Edinburgh University Press, 1942), pp. 7–11 and passim.

37. Parr to Suffolk, *Hamilton Papers*, vol. 1: 8 June 1543, p. 536; 18 July 1543, p. 578.

38. Knox, *Works*, 1:106.

39. Sadler, *Papers*, 1:340.

40. Stage directions in Bannatyne MS., version in Hamer, ed., *Works*, 2:78.

41. Dickinson, *Scotland from the Earliest Time to 1603*, pp. 318–19.

42. Pitscottie, *History and Chronicles of Scotland*, 2:104.

43. Knox, *Works*, 1:104–5; Pitscottie, *History and Chronicles of Scotland*, 2:109–10.
44. Knox's *History*, 1:xxxi–xxxiv. All the prisoners were released, on the intercession of England, by early 1549.
45. Knox, *Works*, 1:171–207; Pitscottie, *History and Chronicles of Scotland*, 2:82–91.
46. Mary to the Duc D'Aumale and Cardinal de Guise, Edinburgh, 12 Nov. 1549. Printed in *Relations Politiques de la France et de L'Espagne avec L'Écosse au XVIᵉ siècle*, ed. Alexandre Teulet, 5 vols. (Paris; Libraire de la Société de l' histoire de France, 1862), 1:201.
47. Knox, *Works*, 1:215.
48. Pitscottie, *History and Chronicles of Scotland*, 2:101.
49. *The Tragical Death of David Beaton* (London: Day and Seres, [1548?]), STC no. 15683, fol. A1ʳ (hereafter cited as Day's edition). My citations are taken from this; references to the comparable passages in Knox, Pitscottie, and Foxe appear for the reader's convenience. All three base their account on the Day edition.
50. The dates of the martyrdoms listed here are those of Knox and Foxe. According to Laing (Knox, *Works*, 1: 61 n), the exact dates "in many instances cannot be ascertained." Cf. Donaldson, *Scotland: James V to James VIII*, p. 54.
51. This definition of *veritie* appears in Alexander Seytoun's letter to James V, as quoted by Knox, *Works*, 1:50. Seytoun wrote the letter from England, after he had escaped the heresy accusation pending against him.
52. Knox, *Works*, 1:65.
53. Day's edition, fol. D5ᶜ–D5ᵛ; Foxe, *Acts and Monuments*, 5:629: Pitscottie, *History and Chronicles of Scotland*, 2:63; Knox, *Works*, 1:154–55.
54. Knox, *Works*, 1:240.
55. Hamer, ed., *Works*, 3:152.
56. Knox, *Works*, 1:186.
57. Foxe, *Acts and Monuments*, 5:626.
58. Day's edition, fol. D4ᵛ–D5ʳ. Foxe, *Acts and Monuments*, 5:629; Pitscottie, *History and Chronicles of Scotland*, 2:62; Knox, *Works*, 1:154.
59. Day's edition, fol. D4ᵛ–D5ʳ. Foxe, *Acts and Monuments*, 5:629; Pitscottie, *History and Chronicles of Scotland*, 2:62; Knox, *Works*, 1:154.
60. Day's edition, fol. F1ᵛ–F2ʳ. Pitscottie, *History and Chronicles of Scotland*, 2:75; Foxe, *Acts and Monuments*, 5:634; Knox, *Works*, 1:167–68.
61. Knox, *Works*, 1:61. 44.
62. Foxe, *Acts and Monuments*, 5:623–24.
63. Knox, *Works*, 1:58–60.
64. Ibid., pp. 43–44.
65. See *The Catechism of John Hamilton*, ed. Thomas Graves Law.
66. Foxe, *Acts and Monuments*, 5:638.
67. See chapter 1.
68. Buchanan, *Rerum Scoticarum Historia*, bk. 15, par. xxix.

69. Foxe, *Acts and Monuments*, 5:637.

70. Ibid., p. 622. Knox repeats the proverb in another context when discussing a "servand to the Bishope of Dunkell, who nether knew the New Testament nor the Old" (*Works*, 1:97).

Chapter 3

Theme

The peculiar relationship of Lindsay's play with the politics of its time requires a definite decision on the play's date if one is to see its association with contemporary Scotland, an association that lends point and immediacy to the substance of the play. Yet, such materials—necessary as they are—cannot alone suffice. Men of all eras have complained against unjust government, but their complaints do not take the same form. Ideas, like language, shift and change, and the writer who today assumes his audience will understand his reference must risk, in years to come, the obscurity which time inevitably brings to all human products. If we are to see *Ane Satyre of the Thrie Estaitis* as a serious exercise of the craft which creates art, we must also view the play within the terms of its own artistic order. We must search for those ideas which Lindsay clothed and used to express his view of contemporary society.

Simply stated, the *Thrie Estaitis* is built, not on the temptation and fall of a king, but on the basic antagonism between reason and sensuality, as that antagonism affects society. This is not a simple dualism, a choice of lust or logic, heaven or hell. This is a matter of serious earthly concern, for the choice of sensuality can lead to the social disorder which destroys justice and in turn brings earthly wrath and ruin to individual men.

The theme is, of course, ancient and multifarious: references to the danger of sensuality are scattered throughout the literature of the Middle Ages. It is most clearly stated, however, in the debate between the civilized beauties of courtly love and the debasement of sensual love which is at least as old as the *Romance of the Rose*.[1] While Lindsay's

Sensualitie is endowed with the trappings and rhetoric of courtly love, the dramatist has framed her nature within another tradition. She is a follower of Venus as seen through Diana's eyes in the allegory *Reason and Sensuality*, and her character reflects the qualities described in Lydgate's version of Guillaume de Deguileville's *Pilgrimage of the Life of Man*.[2]

In the latter, Venus appears in all her foulness, wearing a painted mask to hide her ugly face, riding on a boar. She has been described previously as a huntress, the worst enemy of pilgrims whose only defense is to "eschewe place and syht, / And alway tak the to the flyht. / Tourne thy back, & she wyl go; / And yiff thou flest, she fleth also" (lines 8183–86). She is always in transit, "now in towne, now in the ffeld" (line 13340) and her worst enemy is Chastity whom she and her followers defame "by som sclaundre ffalsely ffounde, / Hyr goode name to confounde" (lines 13191–92). In *Reason and Sensuality*, Diana acknowledges Venus's physical beauty, but describes her actions in the same terms. She is "debonayre vnto the syght, / Lusty, fresh, and amerouse / But in werkyng venymouse, / Full of chaunge and variable" (lines 4057–61). She is "queynte of array" (line 1556), and holds all classes, "both gentil and vileyn" (line 3126), bound in "the girdel of fals lust" (line 1321). As in the *Pilgrimage*, Nature warns the dreamer in *Reason and Sensuality* against the sensual life:

> lyche as reson
> Unto vertu ay accordeth,
>   So sensualyte discordeth,
> And hath noon other appetit
> But in bodely delyt,
> Al set to worldly vanyte

(Ll. 776–81)

Lindsay's Dame Sensualitie follows this tradition. She is indeed beautful in appearance, but her beauty is the beauty of a courtesan who dresses with vanity in "the new gyse" (line 203) and, at her first appearance, vaunts her uncovered head and exposed breasts, while proclaiming the extent of her experience and travels among the kings of Christendom and the papal Court of Rome.

Once a man is caught by this passion, he is lost to good, a view already suggested by the opposition of Venus or Sensuality to Chastity or Reason. Stephen Hawes includes this view in the *Example of Virtue*, and John Rolland provides a more detailed description in the

Court of Venus[3] when Vesta, the defender of chastity, describes the effects of passion:

> of luf the rampand rage,
> The ardent lust, and the kindilland curage,
> The naturall cours, and eik the sauage blude
> Will caus ane man dekay into dotage,
> Vnto the time that the lust he assuage:
> And takis no thocht to ressoun, nor to gude.
>
> (Ll. 388–93)

This sort of passion, Vesta tells her auditors, caused Solomon to tolerate idolatry. Lydgate links the passion with the powerful, too, when the Pilgrim watches Venus and her follower, Gluttony, attack a lord, bind him, and drag him through the mud. Meanwhile, the lord's retainers stand by and do nothing, and the narrator comments that they are people who stood "with hym in ryht and wrong, / With false behestys . . . / In al hys werkys make hym bold / That they wolde with hym abyde / ffor lyff or deth, on euery side" (*Pilgrimage*, lines 13634–39).

Such is the situation of Rex Humanitas. Like Lydgate's lord, when the king is tempted by his retainers, Placebo answers his objections with false assurance:

> Beleiue ȝe that we will begyll ȝow,
> Or from ȝour vertew we will wyle ȝow,
> Or with euill counsall overseyll ȝow
>   Both into gude and euill?
> To tak ȝour graces part wee grant
> In all ȝour deidis participant,
> Sa that ȝe be nocht ane ȝoung sanct
>   And syne ane auld deuill.
>
> (Ll. 227–34)

Urged on by his courtiers, the king falls, as Solomon did, into the passive tolerance of evil, a condition signified by his easy credulity with Flatterie, Falset, and Dissait, and his blind acquiescence to Sensualitie's hatred for Chastitie.

Thus, Lindsay's Sensualitie, for all her easy charm, is essentially the natural daughter of the Venus portrayed in homiletic allegory. As such, her presence explains, for an audience familiar with that tradition, both the vices which surround the king, and the process of his degradation. It was an old and familiar view of human nature, a view which Lindsay joins to an implicit condemnation of courtly love. As C. S. Lewis demonstrates, delight in the fantasy of love waned through the fifteenth century and was replaced by a view which limited love to nonsexual or marital relationships.[4] Lindsay undoubtedly shared this attitude, for he comments in his own romance, *Squire Meldrum*, that Guenevere, Lancelot's love, "was ane Adulterair" (line 54), and that "Of sic amour culd cum na gude" (line 64). In the *Thrie Estaitis*, he underlines this attitude by wrenching the old conventions of romance out of their natural context and thrusting them into collision with the hard light of day. Sensualitie, he leaves no doubt, is a whore, albeit the sort usually named politely "courtesan." The "ladies" in her train are not ladies at all but women of a more common caste, and one, Fund Jonet ("foundling Janet"), implies, in her masculine voice, a bit of perversion (see 335–40). But the real thrust appears in Lindsay's brief use of the courtly conventions. The names of Sensualitie's maids, Danger and Hamliness, date back to the *Romance of the Rose*, where they were used for qualities accorded to the Lady. The character of Danger is particularly ironic in this new context, for instead of being the powerful, male antagonist who must be slain before the lover can hope for intimacy, Lindsay's Danger is a cynical slut who shrugs off her name in a short speech (lines 299–300) and joins in a song to Venus. Hamliness is not a quality which admits the lover to his lady's friendship, but a wench who indulges his vicious tendencies and, on the literal level, distracts the king's courtier with vulgar conversation and ready consent while they wait for their betters to complete their facile bargain. Beyond these touches, Lindsay endows the principals with the rhetoric of courtly love. Sensualitie makes the conventional vow to Venus (lines 499–505) and addresses the prince with elaborate courtesy. The king replies in kind, but Lindsay twists the last line of his speech into a plain expression of lust and leaves no doubt that the rhetoric is only a quick prelude to a common business:

> Welcum to me peirless in pulchritude,
> Welcum to me thow sweiter nor the Lamber,
> Quhilk hes maid me of all dolour denude,
> Solace, convoy this Ladie to my chamber.

> (Ll. 530–33)

While Sensualitie with her attending vices controls the action of part 1, the virtues introduce the themes which receive their fullest treatment in part 2. As sensuality was presented in homiletic allegory as that aspect of Venus which was the mother of all vices, so chastity, in the same tradition, is presented as its opposite: an essential concomitant of virtue and the life of reason. This concept receives its fullest allegorical expression in *Reason and Sensuality* where Diana, the virgin goddess, contrasts the life of reason in her forest, eternal and exempt from change or duplicity, with the eternal mutation and deceitful appearance of existence in the garden of pleasure. But other writers use the contrast to express variations of the same theme: Dame Clenness represents the concept of chastity in the *Example of Virtue*; Vesta, in the *Court of Venus*. And the sinner, King Hart, names chastity in his last testament and sums up her traditional character:

> To Chaistite, that selie innocent,
> Heir leif I now my Conscience, for to scour
> Off all the wickit roust that throw it went
> Quhen sco for me the teiris doun culd powre.
> That fayr sweit thing, bening in everie bour,
> That never wist of vyce nor violence,
> Bot euirmore is mareit with mesour
> And clene of Lustis curst experience.[5]

In the *Thrie Estaitis*, we can see this opposition of chastity and sensuality employed in the grouping of characters. In a pattern of polarity, Chastitie appears with characters usually associated with her—Veritie, Gude-Counsall, and Divine Correctioun, the emissary of God—just as Sensualitie gathers about her the appropriate vices—Wantoness, Placebo, Solace, Flatterie, Falset, and Dissait. Like Sensualitie, Chastitie is not simply an attitude toward sexuality, but is symptomatic of the moral condition in general. Once Lindsay has demonstrated that all the estates of the realm have rejected the life of chastity, the audience knows that the earlier appearance of Veritie in such a land is futile. Lindsay does not have to treat Veritie separately nor endow her with a separate set of scenes. He uses the rejection of Chastitie to show the inacceptability of all virtue to a people who refuse to control the sensual life.

Here, too, the author introduces variations in his portrayal of the virtues. His use of the plain, "godly" rhetoric serves to underscore the Lutheran character of Veritie who, in the Christian tradition, was one of "the four Daughters of God." [6] But he has also reversed the usual relationships of the virtues. In the allegories which we shall discuss later, the virtues are ordinarily the instructors and guides of the pilgrim. They are the beings who interpret the world and who protect the pilgrim from the extreme attacks of the vices. Such is the function of Gracedieu in the *Pilgrimage*, of Sapience in the *Example of Virtue*, of Vesta in the *Court of Venus*. Here, however, Veritie, Chastitie, and Gude-Counsall (he would be called Sapience in a nonpolitical context) are the wanderers and exiles. They are the pilgrims in a dark land who find no one to comfort them. It is from this point of view, the virtues as pilgrims, that the character and appearance of Divine Correctioun takes its literary rationale. In the play, the virtues undergo an experience like that of the pilgrim who is attacked by Sensuality, and, as in a pilgrimage, the emissary of God arrives not, in this case, to save a human soul, but to protect and foster the very existence of the virtues themselves. In terms of the tradition, Divine Correctioun is not a *deus ex machina*, a term applicable to a drama based on probability, but an allegorical representation of God's concern for the virtuous, and the embodiment of the divine intervention which Christianity saw in human history.

We can see, then, that Lindsay both uses and varies the structural conventions of allegory. The apparent protagonist, Rex Humanitas, is not a protagonist in the modern sense at all, and the real action or argument of the play's first part is based, not on the development of character, but on the presentation of the basic antagonism between reason and sensuality, represented by opposing character groupings. Certainly, Lindsay uses the *personae* (or qualities) traditionally associated with this debate, but he changes them to suit the times. He makes Sensualitie a prototype of courtly love, and Veritie, a Lutheran lady. He casts the Virtues, Chastitie and Veritie, as pilgrims while the "protagonist" (the king) represents the goal, not the suffering wanderer. The divine guardian functions as the traditional allegorical protector who, in this play, must rescue the virtues themselves. This "morality play," then, is as much an allegory as its narrative predecessors and contemporaries. It shares with them a set of literary practices and assumptions which our modern world, in some measure, has forgotten.

Until now, we have considered the play in its more general character as moral allegory, an approach which locates the basic meaning of character and action. But aside from an initial description of the topic, we have not looked at its political allegory. While the long history of contrast between sensuality and chastity usually described general aspects of human experience, these qualities were also relevant to political life. Surely it is no accident that two of the virtues Lindsay chose to portray have such relevance. In the medieval analysis of philosophy, *policia* was one of the three realms of practical action, and the virtues usually associated with the art of governing well were *largitas, justicia, pietas, veritas,* and *castitas.*[7]

While the first half of the play is based upon the conflict between chastity and sensuality, as it affects the head of state and thus the state itself, Lindsay shifts the terms of his argument in the second half. To understand the forces operating here, we shall turn our attention to texts which consider the political state. The abstract rules of kingship were embodied in those royal handbooks often modestly named the *De regimine principum*, rules which Lindsay himself recommended to his royal master in the *Dreme* and in the *Complaynt*. In such treatises, the prince is warned he must be morally upright, wary of flatterers, and zealous in heeding the advice of good counselors. But to proceed beyond the simplicites of good advice which, at best, provide mere clues to the action of the play, we will turn also to those texts of the late Middle Ages which show us kings in action and the effects of action on the well-being of the state. From this, we shall see that Flatterie, Falset, and Dissait, the feigned friars, share Sensualitie's role as corrupters of the state and that, in the second half of his play, Lindsay supplants them with their more literal representation, the clergy, and uses the traditional, simple man, Johne the Common-Weill, to sound the themes of Veritie and Chastitie.

We will find through the traditional texts that the concepts of politics and of religion advanced in Lindsay's play are by no means revolutionary.[8] As it is with so many texts of historical importance, the *Thrie Estaitis* exists as a statement of ideas current for several generations and has received its reputation as Reformation literature, not so much for the character of its ideas, as for the fact that those ideas were once again enunciated during a time when the church was beginning to shift from an internecine battle with definite possibilities of conciliation to the monolithic positions of separatism which emerged as the Council of Trent (begun in 1545) gradually chose reaction over conciliation. The Scottish church itself had just closed a provincial council in January which, officially at least, called for many of the clerical reforms which Lindsay espoused. In June, 1552, no man could foresee that the proposed reforms would prove to be meaningless and that by 1559 the nation, once again governed by an inept ruler, would begin to develop a new covenant and a more radical means of reformation. The *Thrie Estaitis* has been viewed as a harbinger of the Reformation, as indeed in many respects it is, but we shall see that it is just as certainly an enunciation of the old moral-political themes which nurtured the best of the old church as well as the new.

Concern for the proper moral character of kings was a central question in the political philosophy of the Middle Ages.[9] That concern continued through the sixteenth century even while the parliamentary system was emerging in England.[10] Throughout the period, it was embodied on a less philosophical level in those handbooks for rulers whose direct history stretches back to the twelfth century.[11] During Lindsay's time, the Scottish reader had a ready source of such reading. He could use the *Secreta Secretorum* in Lydgate's translation,[12] Thomas Hoccleve's *Regement of Princes*,[13] or he could turn to the famous treatise Erasmus wrote in Latin for the instruction of a modern emperor, Charles V. Lydgate and Hoccleve's works are the major representatives of the English tradition, but the Scottish dialect has its sources as well: Gilbert de la Haye (fl. 1456) translated the *Secreta* as the *Buik of the Governance of Princis*,[14] and in 1556 the *Compendious Tractate*, written by William Lauder, was published.[15] The themes also occur in a short poem inserted at the end of the *Liber Pluscardensis* and thought to have been composed about 1460. This "De Regimine Principum Bonum Consilium" was copied into Maitland's Folio and appears in the Fairfax and Marchmont manuscripts as well, a fact which speaks for its currency in the sixteenth century.[16]

While these small texts are useful introductory sources, it is perhaps more instructive to see the principles they enunciate emerging in other, more ambitious works. In two of the more important books of the time, we see the link between the unalloyed teaching of the treatises and the pleasure provided by merging history and literature: Lydgate's *Fall of Princes* (1431–38) and Sir Thomas Elyot's *The Governor* (1531). In book 1, Lydgate tells us that Humphrey, duke of Gloucester, ordered him to translate Boccaccio's book because it was "onto pryncis gretli necessarie / To yiue exaumple how this world doth varie" (1.426–27), and that the duke further directed him to compose an envoy after every book which would

> At the ende sette a remedie,
> With a lenvoie conueied by resoun.

And afftir that, with humble affeccioun,
To noble pryncis lowli it directe.
Bi otheres fallying [thei myth] themsilff correcte.

(2.150–54)[17]

A hundred years after Duke Humphrey saw the *Fall of Princes* as a more detailed instruction in the art of governing, Elyot organized his *Governor* along the traditional lines exemplified by Erasmus's book. Elyot presents his program, not for the education of·kings alone, but as a model for the training of all those properly expected to exercise political power. While his scope is smaller and more tightly organized, Elyot, like Lydgate, maintains a balance between precept and example. It is as if he had taken the best of both traditions: the smaller scope of the handbooks for princes, and the greater liveliness and interest of *exempla* collections.

The material for Lindsay's play comes from this tradition as well as from the reason-and-sensuality allegories. The concept of kingship reveals the principles which support the drama as a single work of art. Although characterized by shifting episodes, the play is held together by repeated themes quite comprehensible and commonplace within the context of contemporary political attitudes. Lindsay's familiarity with this tradition is certain. In the *Dreme*, he exhorts James V to follow the rules of governing; in the *Monarche*, he writes his own chronicle, using traditional examples of kingship and, indeed, referring to "Boochas" and Erasmus, among others.[18] In the play itself, King Correctioun refers to Lucrece and Tarquin, Sardanapalus, and Noah (lines 1753–68, 1697–1705)—all examples where God punishes rulers for the sin of sensuality. Gude-Counsall himself recommends the reading of "the Chroniklis" to the reformed Rex Humanitas (lines 1896–99).

While the allegories we discussed earlier explore the nature of reason and sensuality as it affects humankind in general, the social critics reveal the theme's relationship to the health of the social system which, in feudal relationships, is the direct result of the king's character. The dangers of royal sensuality are fully expounded in the *Fall of Princes*, and the topic is the focus of book 3. There, Boccaccio had asserted the moral responsibility of man and, in a series of tales taken from classical and biblical history, demonstrated the national catastrophe which ensues when a prince is ruled by sensuality. The theme is most clearly enunciated in "The Complaynt of Bochas Oppon þe

luxurie of Princis by examplis of diuers myschevis" (line 1149 ff.).
Here the author explains the nature of "Ladi Resoun" (line 1345 ff.)
and contrasts the concept with the bestial life of sensuality. The sensual life is not "natural" to man whose nature rests in God's gift of
reason, a gift denied to the lower orders of creation. The consequence
of royal bestiality is catastrophic:

> For wher that God list punshe a man off riht
> Bi mortal suerd, farwell al resistence:
> Whan grace faileth, awey goth force & myht,
> Feblith off pryncis the magnyficence,
> Chaungeth their power into inpotence
> Reuersith the kynges ther statli regalie
>
> (Ll. 1457–62)

But it is not only the king who suffers the penalties of his sin; the
people he rules are drawn along the self-same path. Lindsay makes a
glancing reference to this familiar doctrine in the *Dreme* when he
declares that "quhen the heddis ar noch delygent, / The membris
man, on neid, be necligent" (lines 881–84). But it is Erasmus who
provides a most graphic description of the results:

> The corruption of an evil prince spreads more swiftly and widely than
> the scourge of a pestilence. ... The common people imitate nothing
> with more pleasure than what they see their prince do ... under an
> epicure, all disport is wasteful luxury; under a debauché, license is
> rampant. ... No comet, no dreadful power affects the progress of
> human affairs as the life of the prince grips and transforms the morals
> and character of his subjects.[19]

This is the general doctrine, and Lauder, writing in the midst of the
Scots struggle for reformation, preaches on the old theme as well.
With this difference, however: like Lindsay, Lauder prescribes the
preaching of "Goddis wourd of verytie" as the necessary condition for
the heaven-blessed rule of society:

> The Leigis of the Ungodlie kyng
> In daylie trubbyll thay sall ryng;
> For thay tak nother tocht nor cure
> But reuth for to oppresse the pure.
> Thay haue nocht God before thare Ee,
> Bot seruis thare Sensualytie:

And swa that realme is neuer at rest;
Bot styll the pure ar sore opprest.
  Thus without kyngs Y-groundit be
  In Goddis wourd of verytie;
Thare Leigis, also godlie men,
Doand goddis wourd parfytlie ken;
And but trew precheours; I mak plaine,
All Realmes sall underly gret paine,
And sall nocht mys the scurge and rod
Off the hie puissant and mychtie god.

(Ll. 183–98)

Whether Lauder was familiar with Lindsay's work or not, this passage, taken with Erasmus's description of the link between king and people, seems to summarize Lindsay's play about a Scotland governed by an ungodly king. But attribution of direct influence is both dangerous and unnecessary, for the theme seems omnipresent in one form or another. Here is Lydgate's excoriation of the sensual condition:

It is in erthe oon the moste pereilous thyng,
A prynce to been off his condicioun
Effemynat, his wittis enclynyng,
Be fals desirs off fleshli mocioun,
to put hymselff vnder subieccioun,
And thralle his resoun, tresour most precious,
To onleeful lustis, hatful & lecherous.
. . . .
There is the sentence ful pleynli in menyng:
Where women haue the dominacioun
To holde the reyne, ther hookis out castyng,
That sensualite ha[ue] iurediccioun
To entre on resoun bi fals intrusioun,
Werre ageyn vertu most contagious,
To be venquyssid off lustis lecherous,—
It taketh from men ther cleernesse off seyng,
Causeth gret siknessis and corrupcioun,
And to al vertu it is grettest hyndryng

(Ll. 1611–27)

"Where women haue the dominacioun"—we have understood the character of Lindsay's Lady Sensualitie clearly enough from the narrative allegories, but, with the political tracts, the meaning and function of Chastitie's encounter with the tradesmen takes on clarity. With this sequence, Lindsay dramatized the process Erasmus described. Granted, the episode is another example of the proverbial sexual debilities satirized in William Dunbar's "The Sowtar and Tailyouris War" and in his "Amends to the Telyouris and Sowtaris," but, in context, it carries much more weight in the play's structure than the simple exposure of two pseudo geldings. What we should see is that when Chastitie seeks lodging with each of the three estates she finds all classes infected with the same irresponsbility that dominates the court. When, ironically, she finds a resting place, it is with two tradesmen representing the group long ridiculed for their lack of sexuality. Yet, despite their incapacities, even they are not completely free from the reflection of the court, for they invite her to play "cap'out," the drinking game that began the dalliance between Hamliness and Wantoness. Worse yet, their simple impulse toward hospitality is destroyed by two brawling harridans who do indeed "haue the dominacioun." They are Sensualitie's representatives among the Commons, and their victorious excursion to the tavern recalls the first appearance of Sandie Solace, drunkenly rolling into court from a long spree "drinkand into the burrows toun" (line 94). All Scotland is ruled by sensuality, and, in the process, the nation mimics the court until all men are "effemynat," and women rule where reason is unknown.

This interpretation may strike the reader as a rather heavy-handed explanation of what is, after all, a sort of Punch-and-Judy show. Of course, we have a good hearty laugh at the spectacle of two ineffectual little men bombarded by two enormous amazons who are nevertheless afraid of frogs, though bold enough to lift their skirts whenever it is convenient. But the context of the scene changes the total effect, and Lindsay mixes with its sheer burlesque the clergy's parallel refusal of Chastitie, recalled by Taylor's and Sowtar's rueful remark that priests and bishops are right to find their pleasures outside marriage. This, in turn, is a repetition of the courtiers' argument that lechery is no sin, since all the clergy from Rome to Balmerino practice it. Nor should we forget the long tradition of satire against women which flourished in the popular literature of sixteenth-century Britain.[20] In *Eleanor Rummyng*, for example, John Skelton describes a crew of alehouse cronies who would have been no strangers to our tradesmen's wives. Yet for all the hearty humor of Skelton's merry sots, the poet ends his poem with condemnation:

Ebria, squalida, sordida foemina, prodiga verbis,
Huc currat, properet, veniat! Sua gesta libellus
Iste volutabit: Paean sua plectra sonando
Materiam risus cantabit carmine rauco.[21]

We moderns may laugh at the fortunes of Sowtar and Taylor, but we should not forget that their Judys are not puppets but representations of Scotland's sorry state.

It is one of the small ironies of literary history that Lindsay has so often been reproved for "a humour that sinks too often to mechanized dirt," [22] despite the fact that his play's complete title is *Ane Satyre of the Thrie Estaitis in commendation of vertew and vituperation of vyce*. Part of the reason for this unbalanced opinion (aside from the influence of Victorian notions of linguistic decorum which linger still) is the failure to analyze the substance of Lindsay's ideas beyond the scattered attacks reflecting the influence of the Reformation. Thus far, our analysis has emphasized the nature and function of sensuality, as that concept is reflected in Lindsay's representation of king and nation, but, having analyzed our foil, we shall now turn to the "commendation of vertew." Earlier, we saw that Chastitie, as a fictional character, emerges from the traditional opposition of reason and sensuality, but we must examine the other major theme, the nature of justice, to see how Veritie, Gude-Counsall, Divine Correctioun, Pauper, Johne the Common-Weill, and the Doctour of Divinitie also assert the positive values and act as Lindsay's spokesmen for virtue.

In the sixteenth century, the function of the king remained essentially the same as it was for centuries past. That function is expressed in the Virgilian topos: "parcere subjectis et debellare superbos." Such a simple principle appears in Lauder's *Tractate*, joined with the traditional appeal for equitable judgment:

> And kyngs suld heir the pure mans crye
> And helpe thame, rather, in distres,
> Nor thame that hes the gret ryches.
> *To ponysche Vice, and treit virtew,*
> *That is ane Prencis office dew.*
>
> (Ll. 24–28; italics mine)

While Lauder's is the most contemporary Scots reference, we find the same principle emphasized in Gilbert de la Haye's translation.[23] Justice is the single quality which marks the king as king. It is his most important single trait for "quhat prince or king that has nocht this soverane vertu in dede and in herte, he is nocht king na prince, bot he is contrarious to kingis and princis. For proprietee is to king or prince to be just, or ellis he declynis fra the proprietee of princehede, and fra the glorious God of quhom he tuke that office." [24] Elyot begins his third book with the same topic, and in the third chapter adds a further dictum on the conditions necessary for the existence of justice. "Reason," he begins, "societie called company, and knowledge remayninge, Justice is at hand, and as she were called for, ioyneth her selfe to that company . . . whereby hapneth . . . a vertuous and most blessed conspiracie" (3.3.201).[25] Here, too, Elyot contrasts reason and sensuality, and in the next chapter, "Of fraude and disceyte, whiche be agayne Justyce," he explains the nature of truth:

> For unto hym [God] nothing may be acceptable wherin lacketh verite, called communely trouth, he him selfe being all verite, and all things contayning untruthe is to him contrarious and aduerse. And the deuill is called a lyer, and the father of leasinges. Wherfore all thinge, which in visage or apparaunce pretendeth to be any other than verely it is, may be named a leasinge; the execution whereof is fraude, which is in effecte but untrouthe, enemie to trouth, and consequently enemye to god. For fraude is . . . an euill disceyte, craftely imagined and deuised, which, under a colour of trouth and simplicite, indomageth him that nothing mistrusteth. *And because it is euill it can by no meanes be lefull; wherfore it is repugnaunt unto justice.* (3.4.216–17; italics mine.)

Deceit or fraud, then, is a quality antipathetic to truth, antagonistic to God himself, and in both capacities, destructive of justice. It is an attitude Lauder displays in his discussion of temporal judges when, in a line that seems to echo the names of Rex Humanitas's ministers, he says that the king's appointees should be free "frome flattrie, falset, and dissait" (line 457).

Before we examine in detail the use of these concepts in *Ane Satyre*, we can profit from a fictional portrayal of the judgment of a just king.[26] The statement of these themes reverberates through that great English vision, *Piers Plowman*. Appropriately enough, the poem appeared in print before its modern editors again rescued it from obscurity. Robert Crowley produced an edition in 1550 as part of that brief flurry of Protestant-inspired printing during Edward VI's reign.[27] Of course, we have no evidence that Lindsay ever saw a copy in manuscript or in print, but Langland's panorama towers in the history of English social criticism and, as such, is encyclopedic in the resources it provides for study. While we shall do it far less than justice here, we can use it as a base for approaching the play through Langland's clear presentation of the political condition.

The concept of a just king is as important in Lindsay's play as it is in Langland's first vision. At his first appearance in the *Thrie Estaitis*, Gude-Counsall sounds the theme of proper kingship, just after Rex Humanitas has succumbed to Sensualitie. The old man says:

> For wald this King be gydit ӡit with ressoun
> and on misdoars make punitioun:
> Howbeit I haif lang tyme bene exyllit,
> I traist in God my name sall ӡit be styllit
> Sa till I.se God send mair of his grace,
> I purpois till repois me in this place.
>
> (Ll. 596–601)

But the call for just punishment is premature, as we see when the vices immediately enter, and, in a few brief scenes, easily catch the king in their grasp, and through his willing acquiescence, imprison Veritie and Chastitie. Their easy tyranny stands in stark contrast to a comparable action in passus 2 and 3 of the *Visio*. There, as everyone will remember, the dreamer sees the judgment of Mede, the enemy of Holicherche. She is a lady who has much in common with Sensualitie. Like the daughter of Venus, she is a bastard, familiar to popes, companion to vice: Falsehood and Favel (Flattery) are part of her company. But Langland's king is a responsible ruler and through the course of his judgment we see an earthy struggle enacted between right and wrong as it emerges in the truth of Conscience and the half-truth of Mede. The picture of the good king begins with Theology's objection to Mede's marriage when he asserts the supremacy of truth over the frailities of judges:

> And thou ӡ Iustices iugge hir to be ioigned with Fals
> ӡet beth war of weddyng for witty is Truthe,
> And Conscience is of his conseille and knowedth ӡoe uchone.
>
> (B text, 2.136–38)

The king's character emerges more clearly when he hears of Mede's progress to Westminster from his messenger Sothenesse (Truth). His immediate reaction is an order for her apprehension and a vow of punishment that by its vehemence conveys the king's awareness of the dangers of Mede's companions:

> "Now by Cryst" quod the kynge "and I cacche myȝte
> Fals or Fauel or any of his feres,
> I wolde be wroke of tho wrecches that worcheth so ille
> And don him hange by the hals and all that hem meynteneth."
>
> (2.192–95)

He then explores the nature of Mede's character in open court, and, when Conscience objects to his tendency to agree with Mede's self-characterization, the king withholds judgment until another counselor, Reason, comes to court. Then the king's judgment is completed, not directly on Mede, but on the cause she espouses—her retainer, Wrong. Despite the pleas of his courtiers and demanding only that Clergy and Commons agree, the king rejects undeserved mercy and follows his counselor Reason's advice:

> That I were kynge with crowne to kepen a rewme,
> Shulde neuere wronge in this worlde that I wite myȝte
> Be vnpunished in my powers for peril of my soule.
>
> (4.137–40)

This sequence is, of course, only the beginning of the dreamer's long search for Truth and its answers to the varying character of Mede. The episode suggests, however, that in Lindsay's work, Rex Humanitas's failure is not merely personal sin but an immorality which renders him incapable of executing that "punitioun" or administration of justice which Gude-Counsall calls for. That is the chief function of the king. Unlike Langland's king, Rex Humanitas makes no attempt to examine the nature of the three strangers, Flatterie, Falset, and Dissait, who present themselves at his court, but takes their clerical appearance and their words as truth. He permits them to exercise his functions, to expel Gude-Counsall and imprison Veritie and Chastitie without a hearing. As such he is a laggard king, and, although apparently ignorant of his own sin, he is responsible for injustice through his failure to act. Thus he is "in peril of his soule" not merely as a human being, but as a ruler who neglects his social duty under God. It is under Divine Correctioun that he is forced to see his failure as a king and prompted then to call the parliament.

This hearing, like Langland's judgment of Wrong, is designed to extirpate injustice by meting out the punishment of exile and execution.

Turning to a closer consideration of the play, we can now see that Lindsay clearly enunciates the theme of justice in a series of speeches which, once they are comprehended, fall into a simple pattern. These speeches function as *thematic* soliloquies, in contrast to the soliloquy in later drama which was generally used to express character and emotion. Here, the long speeches enunciate the principles and provide the audience with an intellectual frame for viewing the action. From the beginning, the king is presented, not as an individual character but as the type of kingship, the keeper of justice. In the opening speech of the play, Diligence assures the audience that King Humanitie will ultimately behave as a true king should: "With crown and sword and scepter in his hand, / Temperit with mercie quhen penitence appeiris" (lines 22–23), the picture of temporal authority meting out justice with fairness. His reassurance is immediately followed by Rex Humanitas's prayer, a prayer in which he acknowledges the general responsibility of a king to his God: "Sen throw hes giuin mee dominatioun / And rewll of pepill subiect to my cure, / Be I nocht rewlit be counsall and ressoun, / In dignitie I may nocht lang indure" (lines 86–89). Immediately, however, we see him ruled by Wantoness and Sensualitie. After the seduction is presented, Gude-Counsall enters and asks the audience to consider the necessity for reasonable counselors, joining the case of King Humanitie "Overset with Sensualitie / . . . Throw vicious counsell insolent" (lines 588–90) with the current state of Scotland, but hoping that the king will "be gydit ȝit with ressoun, / and on misdoars make punitioun" (lines 596–97). After this reminder to the audience, the vices are introduced, and the spectators see yet another stage in the decline of kingship. Veritie enters, and her speech takes the form of a sermon, centered on the interpretation of three texts. She begins with the text (which later appeared as the motto on the title page of Lauder's *Tractate*), "Diligite Iustitiam qui iudicatis terram." [28] Here she explains at greater length the relationship between God and king which had formed the basis for Rex Humanitas's first speech. In exhorting the king to virtue, she next touches upon the role of "governours" (line 1048) as exemplars of virtue or of vice. Finally, she introduces the topic which will play a greater role in the second half of the play when she directs her sermon to the "Princes of the Preistis" who share in the moral responsibility of the secular princes (lines 1062–69). After this statement, Lindsay arranges a series of scenes which illustrate the final decadence of kingly justice: the plot and arrest of Veritie by the chief ministers of the realm in collusion with the clerical power, and the moral decline of the three estates who abandon chastity as their betters have already rejected it. At last, we see the final abdication of royal power, when Rex Humanitas permits Sensualitie to order Chastitie's banishment:

> As ever ʒe pleis sweit hart sa sall it be,
> Dispone hir as ʒe think expedient:
> Evin as ʒe list to let hir liue or die,
> I will refer that thing to ʒour Iudgement.
>
> (Ll. 1428–31)

Truly, this is a realm where Sensualitie "holde[s] the reyne," and "woman haue the dominacioun." As for the virtues, they seem to illustrate the text of the *Fall of Princes* where Lydgate describes the realm ruled by unjust judges: "Ther is no mor in this mateer to seyne, / Sauff only this: trouthe stant desloat, / [and] rihtwisnesse to no wiht dar compleyne, / With wrong oppressid, wepyng disconsolat" (lines 3263–66).

Then in a manner no more unusual than the arrival of the U.S. Cavalry in an American western, Correctioun's Varlet arrives to assert the influence of God in human affairs and to announce the imminence of divine justice. After the vices rob their master and flee, Divine Correctioun enters, and once again asserts the theme, quoting as his text, "Beati qui esuriunt et sitiunt Iustitiam" (line 1572). The divine emissary again describes the necessity of good counsel in ruling a realm, this time equating such advice with the consent of "Ane Parleament of the estaitis all" (line 1578). And again the function of a king is described, but this time the contrast of tyranny is added—a relevant description in view of the now-complete presentation of Rex Humanitas's degeneration as a governor:

> Quhat is ane King? nocht bot ane officiar,
> To caus his Leiges liue in equitie:
> And vnder God to be ane punischer,
> Of trespassours against his Maiestie,
> Bot quhen the King does liue in tyrannie,
> Breakand Iustice for feare or affectioun:

Then is his Realme in weir and povertie,
With schamefull slauchter but correctioun.

(Ll. 1605–12)

The king repents: again, Lindsay is not interested in the process, but only in the fact which will form a basis for the second half of the play, and the author ends his "first pairt of our play" with a final plea for justice. Raised to his rightful place, Gude-Counsall takes the text this time, "Initium sapientiae est timor Domini" (line 1875), and returns to the theme of Rex Humanitas's introductory prayer. A king, the counselor preaches, is "bot ane mortall instrument, / To that great God and King Omnipotent" (lines 1878–79), and his principal duty is the execution of justice without partiality, tempered only with mercy. The reward is eternal fame or perpetual shame.

Like Lydgate, Lauder, and Elyot, Sir David Lindsay has written no original philosophical treatise on the nature of kingship. His play employs the age-old ideas surrounding one topic, the king in his function as judge. From the range of eternal sins which may destroy a mortal man whether he exercises the functions of king or tailor, Lindsay selected sensuality as the driving force which destroys justice and threatens to destroy Scotland. *Ane Satyre of the Thrie Estaitis* is not a play about a ruler's fall from grace and subsequent reformation, but a dramatic representation of the effect of sensuality on the administration of justice, told in political terms the sixteenth century took for granted: a king, the nature of his rule, and its effect on the kingdom.

Thus far, however, we have discussed only the first half of the play, and we must turn to the second half to see how Lindsay attempts to achieve a greater unity beyond the simple literalism of cause and result, decadence and reformation, the rather tenuous link which a simple survey of the action produces. After intermission, he presents the second half of his action on a different basis, shifting the conventions which form the terms of his art. The first half was written *per allegoriam* (to borrow a term which we shall explore in the next chapter). In the second half, Lindsay shifts to more literal statement, reversing his emphasis in character selection: in the first part, all the major characters represent abstractions (Sensualitie, the Vices, Chastitie, Gude-Counsall); in the second, these abstractions play a minor part, while the emphasis of the action is placed upon characters who represent types.

In the best dramatic practice, part 2 opens with a bit of stage "business" as the Pauper, apparently appearing out of the audience, breaks into the play and actively resists Diligence's attempts to drive him off. But the scene has thematic function as well as dramatic force, a relationship overlooked by those who regard it as an interlude or curtain raiser. Pauper has just come from Edinburgh where he failed to receive justice both at "sessioun" (civil court) and at "seinʒe" (ecclesiastical court). He is now on his way to Saint Andrews, the chief metropolitan see of Scotland. As Pauper's tale unfolds, the audience is reminded of the play's themes, but this time Lindsay presents his argument by the literal example of one man's experience. As such, the episode is analogous to Lauder's description of "pure playntis that yameris at thi yet, / Quhilkis daily has nocht thair fil of mete, / With wiffis and bairnis swonand for falt of brede: / For quhilk God sal the [the king] chalange of thair ded" (*Tractate*, lines 192–96). When restitution is delayed, Lauder says, God hears the poor "criand vengeance, for falt of lifis fude, / Of the and thine, that revis thaim thus thair gude" (lines 244–45).

The treatment Pauper describes is evidence of the absence of justice in Scotland. His vain hope for justice at Saint Andrews, in turn, provides the occasion for Diligence's cynical laughter at such naïveté (lines 2008–10). The state of the church is in turn more vividly illustrated by Pauper's encounter with the Pardoner, that classic butt of medieval anticlerical satire and Lutheran attack. Both the discussion of clerical morals (lines 2008–33) and the mock divorce of Sowtar and his wife sound the theme of sensuality once more. For these reasons, the sequence is pivotal. It once again enunciates the themes which structured part 1, but, as it evolves, it shifts the focus from the first part's portrayal of the abstract relationships of king and society to an examination of Scotland's problems and Scotland's clergy, the group ultimately responsible for the moral condition of the nation.[29]

The major instrument of that examination is Johne the Common-Weill, a man who knows no other rule than common sense. Such common sense, while a lesser form of intellect than abstract argument, is no less a part of reason and a foe to sensuality. It is Johne in the play's second part who becomes the spokesman for the rule of reason and who protests the abandonment in practice of the principles enunciated by Veritie and Chastitie in part 1. Lindsay had used the honest countryman in his earlier poem, *The Dreme*, but the character was not an original invention by any means. Johne the Common-Weill's lineage stretches back through literature at least as far as Piers Plowman. Over the centuries, Piers was limited to the role Langland gave him in the second vision, that of social critic. This character, turned to stereotype, became the spokesman in satirical poems such as *Pierce the Plowman's Crede, The Plowman's Tale, The Complaint of the Plowman*.[30] He also appears as Jack Upland, Colin Clout, John Bon, and others of that ilk. In general, religion is the object of attack, and the adversary is frequently a friar who embodies all the vices attributed to laggard clergymen. Compared to the contemporary John Bon's ridicule of the mass and the doctrine of transubstantiation, however, Johne the Common-Weill's attack seems moderate.[31] Like the pre-Reformation plowmen, Lindsay's character emphasizes matters of individual morality and generally avoids questions of doctrine except as they affect the moral practices of priests. Indeed, the thrust of his complaint is geared to the vision of the good society where order, reason, and morality dominate the collective life of man.

Johne's position is stated in a long speech (lines 2582–2668) which attacks those who pervert the social order: thieves, unjust judges, and idlers. This is hardly a revolutionary speech. Langland dramatized a social order based on the idea that "qui non laborat non manducet" in the half-acre sequence,[32] and Piers denounced the friars as well as false beggars and idlers. More's *Utopia* begins with a discussion of the social problems resulting from such parasites. Like the others of its kind, Johne's speech sets the principles which form the basis for the succeeding examination of the clergy. The only question is whether or not the Scottish clergy engage in satisfactory work and whether they are justly rewarded for work proper to their class. Under Johne's tutelage, Pauper cites his own experience as evidence that the clergy mercilessly collect more than their just reward, and Sowtar and Taylor provide examples of the worker who knows his trade.

After the initial examination of the clergy (during which Johne is threatened with indictment for heresy until Veritie intervenes), Lindsay stages a brief "contest" between the decadent clergy and the idealized Doctour. While the clergy assert their "consuetude" (custom or tradition), the Doctour responds with a sermon. This sermon, which the clergy ridicule, is the last thematic soliloquy on justice. And it is fitting that here the last should be literally the first principles: "To luife thy God as the fontaine and well / of luife and grace" and "To luife thy nichtbour as thou luifis thy sell" (lines 3497–99). These simple statements, familiar to all of us as the basis of the Christian moral code, were part of a less familiar context in the sixteenth century. In his discussion of justice (part of which was quoted above), Elyot analyzes justice in terms of three components: reason, society, and knowledge. Then, in his description of reason, he sets obedience to the two laws of Christ as a prerequisite for the life of reason (book 3 chap. 3). A variation on this analysis appears in the Scottish "De Regimine" poem:

> Iii maneris ar of Iustice generale
> fyrst to thi god syn to thi awn persoun
> To god thou hald thi hart & consciens hale
> as to thi selfe thou exceid nocht resoun
> Syn do law to pepill & to commoun.
> (Ll. 218–22, Maitland's Folio)[33]

It is indeed a variation, but the emphasis is clear: the king's relationship to God and to himself must be based on love and on reason before he can exercise his proper function in doing justice. The Doctour, then, sounds the themes of justice when he preaches his sermon on the Christian law which describes the relationship between God and man, and man and man.[34] After it, Lindsay quickly ends the essential action of the play with the unfrocking of the deformed clergy and the proclamation of the new laws.[35]

By now it should be evident that *Ane Satyre of the Thrie Estaitis* is indeed a single work and not a collection of "disparate interludes." Its unity is based, not on the presentation of character, but on the exposition of theme, advanced and illustrated by an array of characters and episodes. These elements take their meaning from a context periodically explained and emphasized through the use of thematic soliloquies. Such statements are not mere talk extraneously inserted for the love of moralizing; they form the framework which gives point and meaning to the forces embodied in dramatic action. Once one understands the relevance of sensuality and chastity in their character as symptoms of the social order's nature and as keys to the presence or lack of justice on earth, the play reveals its order. That order is based, not on continuity of character or causal action, but on the continuity of theme. The first part of our play demonstrates the workings of sensuality; the second, the reform and extirpation of that cause. Lindsay might have separated the two parts and called them two plays—an act which might have satisfied later notions of the "well-made play." But such a separation would diminish both halves.

Johne the Common-Weill's complaint would lose much of its force if it lacked the preceding demonstration of social disorder. The first part's analysis of sensuality and justice would stand as a valid statement, but it would lose the specific applications of the second part which bring the point home to Scotland.

Flesh and bone, the *Satyre* is a single body. Existing in a definite historical context, the play comments on contemporary concerns which, at its Cupar performance, had not yet become history. Working within the conventions of his own "modern art," Lindsay used the materials of allegory and of political discussion to create a new work of art. Though the centuries have shifted Western political terms and Western conventions of art, an age which has created a "theater of the absurd" and applauded the strangeness of oriental drama should now possess the breadth and flexibility to see reason and order in the morality play.

NOTES

1. For a recent discussion of the concept of courtly love, see the bibliography and essays in *The Meaning of Courtly Love*, ed., F. X. Newman (Albany: State University of New York Press, 1969), especially those by John F. Benton and Theodore Silverstein.

2. *Reson and Sensuallyte*, ed. Ernest Sieper, Early English Text Society, ex. ser. 84 and 89 (London: Kegan Paul, Trench, Trubner and Co., 1903). The poem (which is unfinished) translates and expands on *Les Échecs Amoureux*. *The Pilgrimage of the Life of Man*, ed. F. J. Furnivall, EETS, ex. ser. 77, 83, 92. For modern research on Lydgate, see A. S. G. Edwards, "A Lydgate Bibliography, 1928–68," *Bulletin of Bibliography*, 1970, pp. 95–98.

3. *Example of Vertue* (W. de Worde, 1510). This was edited by Betty Jean Morley (Ph.D. diss., University of Pennsylvania, 1966; DA 27: 4227A) and by Florence Gluck (Ph.D. diss., Western Reserve University, 1966. DA 27: 3426A-7A). *The Court of Venus*, ed. Walter Gregor, Scottish Text Society (Edinburgh: William Blackwood and Sons, 1883–84). Rolland was a younger contemporary of Lindsay's among the group of writers at the Scottish court.

4. C. S. Lewis, *The Allegory of Love* (Oxford: Oxford University Press, 1958; paperback edition), pp. 232–96.

5. Gawin Douglas, *The Shorter Poems*, ed. Priscilla J. Bawcutt (Edinburgh: Scottish Text Society, 1967), p. 72, ll. 929–36. On the authorship question, see ibid., pp. lxxii–lxxviii. For research on the "Scottish Chaucerians," see Peter Heidtmann, "A Bibliography of Henryson, Dunbar, and Douglas, 1912–1968," *Chaucer Review* 5 (1970): 75–82, and Florence H. Ridley, "A Check-List, 1956–1968, for Study of the *Kingis Quair*, the Poetry of Robert

Henryson, Gavin Douglas, and William Dunbar," *Studies in Scottish Literature* 8 (1970): 30–51. The theme also occurs in Henryson's *Fables*, but his treatment does not lend itself to comparison here.

6. See, for example, the initial dialogue in the *Court of Sapience*, ed. Robert Spindler (Leipzig: Verlag von Bernhard Tauchnitz, 1927). There, Mercy, Trewthe, Ryght, and Pease, the Four Daughters of God, debate the fate of man. See also Hope Traver, *The Four Daughters of God. A Study of the Versions of This Allegory with Especial Reference to Those in Latin, French, and English*, Bryn Mawr College Monographs, 6. (Bryn Mawr, Pa., 1907), and her "The Four Daughters of God: A Mirror of a Changing Doctrine," *PMLA* 40 (1925): 44–92.

7. See John Gower's *Confessio Amantis*, book 7, and Curt F. Buhler's analysis in *The Sources of the Court of Sapience*, Beitrage zur Englischen Philologie, no. 23 (Leipzig: Bernhard Tauchnitz, 1932).

8. See also William R. Barclay's "The Role of Sir David Lyndsay in the Scottish Reformation" (Ph.D. diss., University of Wisconsin, 1956).

9. See R. W. Carlyle and J. A. Carlyle, *A History of Mediaeval Political Theory in the West*, vol. 6, *Political Theory from 1300 to 1600* (Edinburgh: William Blackwood and Sons, 1936), and Otto von Gierke, *Political Theories of the Middle Ages*, trans. Frederick W. Maitland (Cambridge: At the University Press, 1913).

10. See John W. Allen, *A History of Political Thought in the Sixteenth Century* (London: Methuen and Co., 1928), and Franklin Le Van Baumer, *The Early Tudor Theory of Kingship* (New Haven: Yale University Press, 1940), especially chapter 6, "The King's Moral Responsibility." Arthur B. Ferguson explores much of the English political literature in *The Articulate Citizen and the English Renaissance* (Durham, N.C.: Duke University Press, 1965). He begins with Gower and Langland.

11. See Lester K. Born's introduction to his translation of Erasmus's *Education of a Christian Prince* (New York: Columbia University Press, 1936). Born discusses Greek and Latin parallels as well as medieval sources.

12. John Lydgate, *Secrees of Old Philisoffres. A version of the "Secreta Secretorum,"* ed. Robert Steele, Early English Text Society, ex. ser. 66 (London: Kegan Paul, Trench, Trubner and Co., 1894).

13. Thomas Hoccleve, *The Regement of Princes*, ed. F. J. Furnivall, Early English Text Society, ex. ser. 72 (London: Kegan Paul, Trench, Trubner and Co., 1897). Jerome Mitchell's *Thomas Hoccleve* (Urbana: University of Illinois Press, 1968) is the most recent study.

14. See *Gilbert of the Haye's Prose Manuscript*, ed. J. H. Stevenson, vol. 2 (Edinburgh: William Blackwood and Sons, 1914).

15. The full title is *Ane Compendious and Breve Tractate Concernyng the Office and Dewtie of Kingis, Spirituall Pastoris, and Temporall Jugis. (Extant Works*, ed. Fitzedward Hall and F. J. Furnivall, Early English Text Society, orig. ser. 3, 41 [London: N. Trubner and Co., 1870]). Although, strictly speaking, the tract

was published in 1556, four years after the play, I assume it is a reflection of ideas current at the time of the play. Lauder was a younger contemporary of Lindsay's. A native of Lothian, he was educated at Saint Andrews, beginning in 1537, and in the late 1540s and 1550s frequented the court as a writer. He died in February, 1572/73. See preface to *Extant Works*.

16. Poem no. 39 in *The Maitland Folio Manuscript*, ed. W. A. Craigie, vol. 1(Edinburgh: William Blackwood and Sons, 1919), 115–25. Craigie discusses the poem and manuscript problems in 2:73 where he describes the Fairfax version as older than either the Marchmont or Maitland texts. However, the Maitland is the only source for the end of the poem.

17. All quotations from the *Fall of Princes* are from Henry Bergen's edition (4 vols. [London: Kegan Paul, Trench, Trubner and Co., 1918–19]). Like most of Lydgate's work, the *Fall* has suffered from lack of study and oversimplification. For a more balanced view, see Walter F. Schirmer's *John Lydgate*, trans. Ann E. Keep (Berkeley: University of California Press, 1961), and Alain Renoir's *The Poetry of John Lydgate* (London: Routledge and Kegan Paul, 1967).

18. See Hamer's index of Lindsay's references in *Works*, 4:298–302.

19. Erasmus, *Education of a Christian Prince*, trans. Lester K. Born (New York: Columbia University Press, 1936), pp. 156–57.

20. For an exhaustive listing of the texts, see Francis Lee Utley's *The Crooked Rib* (Columbus: Ohio State University Press, 1944).

21. *Works of John Skelton*, ed. A. Dyce, vol. 1 (London: T. Rodd, 1843), p. 115. "Let the drunken, squalid, filthy woman, full of words, run, hurry, come here! This little piece tumbles out her goings-on. This mocking paean sings its subject with her gravel voice and twanging plectrum" (translation mine). The text appears in Philip Henderson's *The Complete Poems of John Skelton, Laureat* (London: J. M. Dent, 1959) but Robert S. Kinsman omits it in his volume *Poems* [of] *John Skelton* for the Clarendon Medieval and Tudor Series (Oxford: Clarendon Press, 1969).

22. Agnes Mure Mackenzie, in her introduction to James Kinsley's edition of *Ane Satyre*, p. 26. My use of her phrase does not adequately reflect her view of the play. I use it, however, because she phrases very nicely one sort of reaction which was typical. I think, or hope, we have got past the point of having to placate such responses.

23. No analysis of specific variations within the history of this idea will appear here. We are only concerned to extract those few simple principles relevant to the play—an attempt to synthesize the thought of the time rather than to analyze. For the latter, see studies such as Allen's *History of Political Thought in the Sixteenth Century* and Baumer's *Early Tudor Theory of Kingship* cited above.

The same theme appears addressed to the king in the Maitland Folio poem: "Reward worthi and punish wikytness, / Nurice vertu, exclude vice and errour" (ll. 22–23).

24. *Gilbert de la Haye's Prose Manuscript*, p. 146.

25. Sir Thomas Elyot, *The Governor*, ed. H. H. S. Croft, 2 vols. (London: C. Kegan Paul, and Co., 1880).

26. This portrayal parallels Lydgate's description in book 1 of the *Fall of Princes*:

> A prynce sholde assemble thyngis tweyne,
> Withynne hymsilff: ful prudently
> Shet up his doomys betwixe lookis tweyne,
> On off the soule, resoun for that party,
> Prudence chose out, and rith for the body;
> And atween bothe, or he yiue a sentence
> To counseil calle trouthe and good conscience.

(1:ll. 4642–48)

27. We shall use here, as Crowley did, the B text (ed. W. W. Skeat, 2 vols. [Oxford: Oxford University Press, 1886]). *Piers Plowman: Critical Approaches*, ed. S. S. Hussey (London: Methuen, 1969) provides an introduction to the extensive scholarship.

28. The title page is reproduced in Lauder's *Extant Works*.

29. We have treated those specific complaints at length in chapter 2 and shall examine the dramatic structure of the play in chapter 5. Here we are primarily concerned with meaning.

30. See Arthur R. Heiserman's *Skelton and Satire* for an analysis of the tradition before *Colin Clout*.

31. *John Bon and Master Parson* was printed in 1548 by Day and Seres who also printed Lindsay's *Tragedie of the Cardinall* in *The Tragical Death of David Beaton*.

32. In his discussion of work, Hunger quotes a comparable text, from Psalm 128: "Labores manuum tuarum quia manducabis; beatus es, et ben tibi erit" (B text, 1:255).

33. In some respects, the sermon is a shorter version of that preached by Holichurche in the *Visio*, passus 1, ll. 139–207.

34. See T. P. Dunning's discussion of this precept as the basis for the just society in his *Piers Plowman: An Interpretation of the A-Text* (Dublin: Talbot Press, 1937), pp. 106 ff.

35. As we shall see in chapter 5, Lindsay ends his play with a long epilogue that functions both as entertainment and as summary.

Chapter 4

Allegory

If history contains the stuff of men's lives, art is the medium through which men understand their lives, seeing reality cast in the images of the past, and casting the present in the old images, selected and refined to mirror more closely the details of their present concerns. As scholars, we attempt to re-create those forms when we study the literature of the past, and, frequently, our work is valuable in proportion to our ability to stand outside our own era and to surmount the limitations which our awareness of modern literature imposes upon us.

With this chapter, then, the second major effort of this small book begins. In the previous sections, I have attempted to develop the range of reference which points up the meaning of the *Thrie Estaitis*. Given what I hope is that new clarity, we may now try another form of analysis which moves away from interpretation or meaning into the consideration of form and the methods artists use to create coherent works of art. What I try to do here is quite simple. It is an attempt to strip away the literary preconceptions with which our education equips us. These preconceptions, hardening into dogma, can prevent us from seeing anything that does not fit our analytic point of view. I have, then, gone back to the simplest questions and tried to answer them in terms of specific materials from a specific time: what is a story? what is a plot? what is a character? what is representation? what, then, is an allegory? My answers are very simple, a simplicity I have cultivated, for too much of our modern discussion of art proceeds in modern allegories, and I would change that, if I could. For myself, an art which fails to communicate with a reasonably intelligent audience is no art, but an exercise in artistic pedantry for a limited audience which deserves what it gets. Art lost in history can be arcane, but that character usually comes from our loss of its cultural environment. Shakespeare, to a child, is gibberish; to an adult, is sublime because the adult has learned how to read that greatest of writers who is a living antique. The scholar, then, is handmaiden (or manservant) to the past: he makes those bare bones live again.

But if we are to flesh the bones of allegory, we must turn from the views that were created by our predecessors. This is not done for the sake of novelty, but from a perception that the great scholarly studies of the immediate past lived within their own era and were formed by the aesthetic attitudes of the first half of the twentieth century. We may be no better, but it is time for new accounts. Perhaps this generation, living among modern allegories, can rediscover the bases of that long tradition of literary allegory which was a major creation of the medieval mind.

But even to use the word *allegory* invites a storm of confusion.[1] The several meanings of the term which have come down to us through history have an august pedigree. In modern medieval scholarship, the dominant use of the term is the oldest: allegory as a form of biblical exegesis, a form that so colored the intellectual habits of the age that it naturally found a place in literature and in the glosses or commentaries (critical editions, if you will) which were created for that literature. In English literature, this form of allegory has been developed and applied by D. W. Robertson and what we may call "the Robertsonian school." Primarily a method of interpretation, it does not concern us here.[2]

My approach is basically a genre approach. However, it does not attempt to isolate common fictional patterns. These have been listed for decades and the terms are well known. Medieval allegories are cast within dream frames, within pilgrimages or journeys, within debates or legal scenes of court or parliaments ("the three estates"), within gardens (classical or medieval or both), within knightly quests, within beast fables, within castle or town or countryside, in heaven or on earth. We all know this. To classify allegories within such groups is suspiciously like making a list. What interests me here is not the similarities of story, but the use of plot and character to create effects on the audience. This is the artistic strategy of a given allegory, and it is the strategy, not the *donnée* or tale, which shapes the work. Quite simply, I find that strategy centered around the thesis and its development through the course of the fable. Such a position cuts across both narrative and dramatic forms which use allegorical statement. It emphasizes similarities between argumentation (essays or orations) and fiction (or what is loosely called "creative writing"). Finally, it considers allegory not as a genre in itself but as a fictional method for telling truths through the use of tales. As a method, allegory may be as small as a figure of speech or a brief variation within a larger whole; or it may be as large as a lyric poem, a narrative, or a drama. The discussion of allegory is primarily a question of its relation to other elements in the individual work. Allegory is a medium for communicating meaning, a means rather than an end in itself.

This essentially expository nature may be the reason why allegory fell out of favor with the old *avant-garde* of this century until the turn that modern taste has taken recently. We seem to be discarding the old aesthetics (created circa 1900–50), but the movement toward a break with the recent past is still mixed and unclear. Our modern taste is still shaped by nineteenth-century realism mixed with the subsequent rebellion in art. We are still accustomed to framing aesthetic questions on the basis of probablility. Given a particular narrative, we are inclined to ask whether the events are convincing in terms of our own concepts of "reality" and whether they grow out of each other in a probable and necessary sequence of cause and effect. Accustomed to regarding fictional characters as representations of individual human beings, we apply our own theories of human behavior and ask questions about motivation and the growth or change of character. This is an entirely reasonable approach for literature such as Shakespeare's plays or Henry James's novels which are mimetic representations of the human situation and human behavior. If, however, we bring these expectations of verisimiltude to allegory, demanding modern psychological causation and motivation, we will naturally find such literature distasteful.

Like others, this examination of allegory is made, not to produce a definitive theory, but to discover those practices of Lindsay's predecessors which explain elements of the *Thrie Estaitis* foreign to the modern aesthetic. The material is selected from the homiletic allegories of the fifteenth and early sixteenth centuries, briefly discussed in chapter 3: Lydgate's translation of Deguileville's poem, *The Pilgrimage of the Life of Man*; Hawes's *Example of Virtue*; *Reason and Sensuality*; the *Court of Sapience*; *King Hart*; John Rolland's *Court of Venus*. On the basis of these poems, I frame a few simple principles which are neither new nor spectacular, which critics have often assumed but seldom enunciated clearly. This, then, is a descriptive effort centered, not on questions of content or of language, but on questions of structure: plot, character, function. Against this background, we turn to four political texts which illumine the *Thrie Estaitis: Piers Plowman* (the first two visions), John Gower's *Vox Clamantis, Mum and the Soothsayer*, and the *Complaint of Scotland*. As a result, we should gain some insight into the artistic assumptions and practices which the play shares with earlier narrative allegory. We shall not "solve" the problem of allegory, but, perhaps, as a by-product, we shall cast a little light in that dark corner.[3]

Most literary historians still regard their duty as done once they have described the journeys of our allegories, a few of the characters, and the quality of the imagery. But this is concentration on the *material* of the allegories: the endless journeys, the coveys of virtues and vices who parade down the road in seemingly endless lines, the doltish pilgrims who are always having to be *told*, like someone endemically endowed with bad manners. While five of the allegories we shall discuss here use a dream or vision frame (*King Hart* does not) and tell of adventures on a fantastic journey, each poem differs in its topic or scope. In the early fifteenth century, Lydgate translated Deguileville's *Pilgrimage*, the longest of the texts we shall consider here. A gigantic work, longer than *Piers Plowman*, the poem is comparable to the others largely on the basis of superficial characteristics. It includes a vision, a naïve traveler, a journey full of incident, a group of helpful advisers, and a collection of grotesques. But while all this is true, this is not the simple battle between virtues and vices, not a psychomachia in Prudentius's manner nor even as it is adapted into the battle between Venus and Pride at the end of the *Romance of the Rose*. As in the morality plays, the Pilgrim is an everyman who is experiencing, not the journey toward death, but life itself, signified by a series of encounters with human temptations. When, as frequently happens, he is in danger of succumbing to those temptations, or of being captured by the vices, he is rescued by his protector, Divine Grace.

By merely examining the kinds of episodes which comprise the action of the *Pilgrimage*, we can see that the poet presents us with a particular view of life and that, long as the poem is, it is a limited view of life. It is not, as *Piers Plowman* is, for example, a picture of court and country with their attendant vices and with a plan for social reformation on the basis of "mede" justly administered. That is a poem more closely geared to group experience and centrally concerned with the social effects of virtue and vice.[4] In contrast, Deguileville limits his topic to one interest, the nature of life as it affects the individual soul; within that broad topic, he centers his emphasis on the nature and depiction of vice. This center of interest becomes more apparent when the *Pilgrimage* is compared to an allegory such as Hawes's *Example of Virtue*, a slighter poem both in length and in art that begins in much the same way. The Dreamer is taken to the dwelling place of Nature, Fortune, Hardiness, and Wisdom, where he learns the various earthly aspects which those ladies control. He then sets out on his journey. But Hawes wastes little time on the portrayal of vice, relegating only one of his fourteen chapters to the temptations, an encounter with Dame Sensualitie and Pride. Emphasizing virtuous action, Hawes examines the nature of experience through the character of Wisdom and the rewards which the youth gains at the Castle of Clenness. (There he is given his name, Vertue, and wed to his lady.) Despite apparent similarities, then, the *Pilgrimage of the Life of Man* and the *Example of Virtue* are quite different poems, sharing some common devices, but reflecting entirely different interests and emphases.

While these two allegories are less closely related in theme than in action, the focus of moral allegory can be much closer than the previous contrast suggests. The *Court of Sapience*, for example, is primarily a work of encyclopedic instruction. The author begins with Sapience's narrative on the nature of man, presented through a debate by the Four Daughters of God, continues with descriptions of the nature of natural phenomena and of the seven liberal arts, and ends with instruction in basic religious truths. Thus, the topic of the *Court of Sapience* is the categories of knowledge, human and divine.[5]

These three poems deal with more complex topics than allegories such as *Reason and Sensuality*, *King Hart*, or the *Court of Venus*. Although he left it incomplete, the author of *Reason and Sensuality* obviously intended to write an allegory based on a simple contrast between the life of Reason (exemplified by the grove of Diana) and the life of Sensuality (exemplified by Venus and the Garden of Love). It is a serious poem, which explores the contrast between two views of human life. John Rolland's *Court of Venus* is another matter. There the same contrast (here embodied in Vesta and Venus) forms the material of the poem, but the author treats the topic as a Valentine Day's amusement. (His comic turn at the end, alas, is not quite successful. Venus has the worst of the argument but still gains the prize, despite logic.) Yet this poem, too, is enclosed in a dream frame and presents many of the same arguments found in *Reason and Sensuality*. Still another problem forms the basis for *King Hart*. Here the author tells of the *physical* life of man through the tale of a king who conquers a castle only to find himself conquered by its mistress, Dame Pleasance. Later, when Age appears, his lady leaves him, and the king (man) finds he must take cold comfort in the spiritual virtues. The emphasis of the poem rests, not on the quality and character of such entities as Chastity and Pleasance (although they are part of the narrative), but on the process of aging which moves a man from the delights of youth to the consequences of age.

When we say that the topics of these poems are less complex, this should not be understood as a statement about the quality of each allegory. It is only a statement about the topic which the poet attempts to discuss. Obviously, poems like the *Pilgrimage of the Life of Man* or the *Example of Virtue* which purport to portray general truths about all human experience, or a poem like the *Court of Sapience* which attempts to engross all knowledge as its subject, attempt themes more intellectually difficult than poems like *Reason and Sensuality* or the *Court of Venus* which deal only with the nature of love, or a short work like *King Hart* which is essentially simple description of the physical process of man's life. The subject itself may be more or less interesting, more or less difficult, but in literature, it is the artistry or handling of the theme that provides the essential material of literary judgment. When we say that a topic is more or less complex, we are making only a descriptive statement. This brief discussion should suggest, however, that on the simple, literal level of thematic choice, the six allegories here discussed are quite different.

Having disqualified some of our aesthetic attitudes which lead to misconceptions about the nature of allegory, we shall now try to describe some of the basic allegorical practices. All allegories have a true beginning and end. They begin with a statement of the problem which is the topic of the poem. This statement may be made in a number of ways. For example, the poet may use an introductory debate, as Rolland did in the *Court of Venus*, or he may suggest his theme through an introductory scene such as the repetition of the choice of Paris in *Reason and Sensuality*. An allegory ends when the problem has been explored to the satisfaction of the author, i.e., when he has presented those aspects of the topic which interest him. If we

take this view, then one of the first questions we ask about an individual allegory is "Given the topic, how has the author treated it?" To
answer that question, we must consider those literary practices or
conventions which are typical in the fifteenth and early sixteenth
centuries and atypical in our own.

One should first recognize the essentially mosaic nature of allegory. The action is not one of complication, of increasing complexity of
conflict. Rather, the action is composed of a series of episodes which
are related by meaning or pattern and not by causation. The Pilgrim
does not meet Sensuality because she is a friend of Pride's and a
member of the same social circle, but because the author is successively examining the various kinds of sin. In other words, the encounters of allegory usually operate by chance in terms of the story: they
are introduced and ended as the author wishes to begin and end his
discussion of a particular aspect of his subject. Allegorical representation, then, tends to be episodic on the level of event. Its episodes are
arranged analytically, in terms of the argument, instead of causally, as
they usually are arranged in representational narrative. For example,
in *Reason and Sensuality*, Diana's discourse on the superiority of the life
of reason and its attendant virtue of chastity is quite out of place if one
simply considers the probable psychological state of the dreamer. The
youth has just repeated the judgment of Paris in his choice of Venus
over Minerva and Juno. Since he is full of illusion about the nature of
love, the conversation is wasted on him, for he understands none of it
nor does it affect in the least his eagerness to visit the Garden of Love.
But, if one sees the poem as a fictionalized argument, this "Judgment
of Paris" becomes a means for introducing the conflict between the
rational and the sensual life. Diana's attempt at persuasion then becomes an exposition of the argument for reason, and prepares *the
reader*, not the dreamer, for a more critical and sophisticated view of
events in the Garden of Love. The position of the Diana episode in
Reason and Sensuality reflects an artistic rationale based on the rhetorical needs of the argument and not on the development of character.

As the structure of allegorical plot is controlled by the demands of
exposition and persuasion (i.e., argument), so character functions as a
counter in the plot. The generalized or "typical" characters do not
confuse the modern reader, trained by comedy to accept with delight
a persona who is all "Shallow" or "Surface" (to indulge in an
Elizabethan pun). But the characters called *abstractions*, the vices and
virtues and concepts (e.g., Grace, Nature) are curiosities which we

tend to dismiss as relics of a naïve age or unfortunate examples of the *deus ex machina*. In our poems, these abstract characters may appear to be human, but they are really extrahuman. In this very special world, the rules of social intercourse are quite informal. The narrator's interest is not in the character of these figures, but in their *qualities*, since they are what they represent: concepts. As such, these static creatures of eternity do not develop or change in their essential nature. Nature can never be anything but Nature, nor Pride anything but Pride. The author does not disclose his personages gradually, expecting us to identify them through their conversation and action, as we learn to know real people. This would be a waste of time, for he expects us to identify them at once as unsavory or admirable characters. As men we have met these "facts" of the moral life, and as readers of allegory we have met these "characters" many times before. We are most interested in what this writer will do with a group of traits and characteristics we already know. Existing outside the real world, these extrahumans announce themselves as soon as they appear and frankly discuss their own characteristics. Since they are not human beings who have to cope with other human beings, and since their existence and natures are eternal, they have nothing to fear and little to gain from the behavior of their auditor. They are forces which may affect the Pilgrim's life, but they themselves can be neither helped nor harmed by human intervention. Literally, they are only concepts; the character represented is the result of iconography; that is, the result of the Christian or literary tradition.

Such characters are also capable of appearing and disappearing, as figures do in a dream or vision. This attribute is particularly characteristic of a frequent character who acts as the dreamer's guardian and guide. Divine Grace fulfills her function in the *Pilgrimage* by providing the Pilgrim with basic instruction at the beginning of his journey. After leaving him to try the road as best he can, she reappears again and again when he is in danger of harm, as grace does indeed come to the reverent Christian in time of temptation. Sapience in the *Example of Virtue* fills the same role; Venus appears unexpectedly to defend her flagging defender in the *Court of Venus* and to punish his blasphemous opponent. The lesser figures enter the scene as casually, too. Age, with Conscience and his band, arrive at the palace of King Hart—not because groups of unexpected guests were a common occurrence in the sixteenth century, but because the poet has completed his description of youth and now marshalls his art to turn our attention to age, for which he invents allegorical equivalents.

Our conceptions of representing time and distance are also quite irrelevant in the allegories. It is certainly a bit discomfiting to find at the end of a comparatively short allegory, the *Example of Virtue*, Youth's announcement: "By this tyme was I lx yere olde." When Dame Plesance leaves him, King Hart returns without warning to the castle he must have left years ago and finds everything there as ready for him as it was before. In the *Court of Venus*, Desperance uses the three-day period between his summons and his required presence at Venus's court to make seven different visits to potential defenders such as the Muses and the Nine Worthies who dwell in scattered places many normal miles apart. Yet Rolland leaves three and a half months between the time when Venus resolves to punish Desperance (February 14) and the time when her sheriff serves the summons (May 28). Since such practices are common in allegory, we must conclude that realistic representation of time and space simply must not be a problem our allegorists took seriously. And why should they? These tales take place outside of time and the realism that concept imposed at a later date when literature narrowed to the analysis of character. Here, if time is at all relevant, it may be signified by a simple narrative bridge, "Next, the pilgrim. . . ." "After a rest. . . ." We know this is a fiction, a fantasy, and any man who, in a dream, may visit the Nine Worthies may do so at his own pace and in his own time.

From this brief discussion of allegory, we should conclude that the critic who demands characterization and verisimiltude from this particular kind of literature is doomed to frustration and subsequent distaste. Episodes are not framed and placed to reflect probability, but to present the reader with parts of the poem's argument in a particular order or for a particular rhetorical effect. Character is not divulged primarily by demonstrated action, but by direct narrative, usually, indeed, by self-description. Individuals appear and disappear at the need of the topic, while time and distance are simply signified in the eternal world of allegory.

Looking at the *Thrie Estaitis* from this point of view, we can see that the play incorporates many of the conventions we have observed in the narrative allegory. Earlier scholars have characterized it as episodic or "formless," but this is a criticism based on the concept of dramatic form as sequential action moving with increasing complications through a climax to the denouement. The *Thrie Estaitis*, however, works from a different concept of unity, the unity of argument, and, while the play does fall into two distinct parts which are marked by an intermission, these parts are integral. The apparent protagonist, Rex Humanitas, is not a protagonist in the modern sense. Rather, like the pilgrim of the allegory, he is a vehicle for the argument. The topic is not a king's biography, but a dramatization of the subversion and subsequent reformation of a kingdom. The king is important, not as an individual soul falling to perdition, but as a political leader whose moral condition determines the state of the nation, and Rex Humanitas is treated as such from his first appearance. From this point of view, part 1 is a description of the progress of decadence, or the causes of the realm's decay, while part 2 demonstrates the means for the removal or reformation of that social and political decadence.

In the depiction of time and space, the first part of the *Thrie Estaitis* is more like *King Hart* than any of the other allegories discussed here. The locale of the play is limited to the court and a vague expanse of countryside around it which may be taken to represent the nation. (Rex Humanitas is not a traveler or pilgrim in the literal sense, but like the pilgrims and like King Hart, he is the naïf, the inexperienced youth who acquires experience. This, however, is the experience of a king, not that of the individual represented as a pilgrim or a monarch.) Yet while the locale is comparatively static, time and space are represented in the same way they are in the allegories. From the text and from what we know of contemporary staging, the actors appear to be positioned at various intervals on the playing field.[6] A change of scene is then represented by a simple shift of the dialogue from one set of characters to another, while the time it takes to travel from one point to another is represented by the character's walking from one group to another. For example, this occurs when Wantoness is sent on his journey to bring Sensualitie to the King, and when Chastitie successively looks for lodging with the various members of the three estates. Such practice is dramatic representation of comparable elements in narrative allegory, as suggested here by our discussion of Rolland's treatment of time and space in the *Court of Venus*.

The characters are static, too. While the rapid character shift depicted in Rex Humanitas's fall from initial grace does occur in the first five hundred lines of the play, one should not regard this as a crude attempt at characterization. So it may appear to those educated by expectations of "proper" motivation and probability, but Lindsay is not attempting to delineate the psychological process of temptation.

He has compressed the process into a series of short scenes which the audience takes as a sign of that process. He is interested, not in the internal process as it affects character, but in the fact of the king's shift to the sensual life which, he demonstrates, is produced by the influence of the courtiers and in turn provides the conditions for the subsequent action which stands for the fact of national decadence.

From this examination of allegory, we see that the apparent disorder of *Ane Satyre of the Thrie Estaitis* is disorder only in terms of modern expectations. In fact, the play reflects the practice of its non-dramatic predecessors in the presentation of topic, character, time, and place. But, so far, we have looked at narrative allegory to see what implicit assumptions the play shares with them in terms of basic artistic practice. Another group of texts supplements comparison with contrast, generalization with differentiation. Earlier, we said the allegories varied across a long range of topics, including the nature of sin, of virtue, of love, of knowledge itself. If we limit ourselves to allegories concerned with political life, we can see that the range of artistic device is wide, even in this limited topical area.

Allegories can be differentiated on the basis of their fictions. One kind of allegory uses a *metaphorical* construction. Here, people can be presented as animals and the resulting story is a beast fable, like that in *Vox Clamantis*.[7] Man is represented as a pilgrim (*Pilgrimage*), a king (*King Hart*), a knight (*Example of Virtue*), and the story is a succession of adventures which convey meaning or a special experience which appears as a specific place or series of places (*Reason and Sensuality, Court of Sapience*). Here, the writer takes the topic or situation which interests him and turns it into a fable which provides the terms for his invention of equivalences.

The metaphorical allegory differs from that based on generalization. This we may call the *literal* allegory. When the writer chooses to discuss kingship, for example, he talks not about a lion or about Mount Olympus, but about a king and his court. It is not an individualized representation of a specific king and his court; it is a generalized representation of a nonspecific king and a nonspecific court—not Richard II or James V, but simply a "Rex Humanitas" or "King." This is a distinction based on the general character of the fiction. It ignores the usual classification based on character types or topic, yet it recognizes basic differences analogous to R. W. Frank's description of allegory as symbolic or personified.[8]

If we interpret allegory along this general metaphorical-literal line, the terms are neither inflexible nor all-inclusive. An individual work may be an allegory, but allegory can also be a rhetorical device subordinate to a different sort of organization. *Piers Plowman* is an allegory: in the whole poem, the commentary is subordinate to, and grows out of, the series of fictions presented. *Vox Clamantis* is not an allegory. It is a complaint, a critical essay in verse, which uses allegory as a device, a means for introducing the reader to the situation and for producing an emotional effect. This is not a matter of essential difference but of proportion. Both Langland and Gower comment on the action they present, but Langland, in general, speaks through the fiction, implying his attitude with comparatively brief commentary while Gower presents his fable for emotional effect while reserving his detailed analysis for the essay which follows it and expands its meaning. Gower speaks directly; Langland, indirectly. Both, however, construct their fables to the requirements of their theme.

The division between fable and exposition in *Vox Clamantis* is not as sharp in *Mum and the Soothsayer*[9] which, nevertheless, employs allegory as a device subordinate to direct exposition. Both writers construct beast fables. Gower tells of the Peasant's Rebellion as an attack by animals whose ferocity, unleashed, infects the domesticated animals, attracts swarms of noxious insects, and turns the entire animal world into beasts of prey bent on the destruction of everything that does not share their viciousness. Playing on our disgust for swarming flies, ravenous oxen, maddened geese, Gower produces loathing for the behavior of the brutalized peasantry and anxiety for a society overturned in chaotic violence. The horror arises from the perversions of the beasts' natures and their parallel to the actions of men who pervert the social order. The author of *Mum and the Soothsayer* uses a different range of meaning for his beast fable. He, too, wishes to tell the events which led to social chaos and the deposition of Richard II. However, he begins with a direct statement of the national condition and introduces his beast fable (passus secundus), not to pose the problem or describe the emotional effect, but to narrate the events which caused Richard's downfall. He deals primarily, not in the connotative meanings of Gower's beasts, but in the denotative meanings of heraldry: Richard is the White Hart; Bolingbroke, the Eagle; Gloucester, the Swan. Both writers use the allegorical beast fable as a rhetorical device subordinate to the structure of the whole poem, but the fables are conceived in different terms—one is connotative, the other denotative—and are introduced at different points in the work and for different purposes.

Mum and the Soothsayer is useful to our analysis for another purpose, too, for the author also creates a literal allegory to account for the king's deposition. In the third passus, he tells in 164 lines (lines 207–371) the story of a court lost in debauchery where Witt, a greybeard in modest dress, is mocked and barred from the court. This action is eventually punished by God, the absolute King who calls his heavenly warriors together and destroys the recreant king and his court. This, too, accounts for Richard's fall, the event which underlies the fable. It illustrates the same theme: the unjust king (the hart) has surrounded himself with unjust retainers (the white harts; the young, debauched courtiers), refused the counsel of the wise (the Swan, Witt), and has been conquered by the agent of a just destruction (Bolingbroke, the Eagle; God, the Heavenly King). Though smaller in scope and less detailed in its analysis, this second, literal allegory operates within the same terms used in the first two visions of *Piers Plowman*. Langland examines the nature of society in the King's court and in the half-acre by generalization, *not* by a system of metaphor. His king, however, *is* ruled by Conscience, Wit, and Reason, a difference in event but not in *kind*. Both the second allegory of *Mum and the Soothsayer* and the first two visions of *Piers Plowman* treat the topics of social order, and both cast their discussions, not in metaphorical terms such as the beast fable, but in generalized representations. The differences within those representations result from the uses of the fiction: the anonymous writer shows the causes of decay in Richard's monarchy; Langland presents us with a picture of the rule of justice which he subsequently elaborates in the half-acre sequence. Both, however, are *literal* allegories, different in their meaning, scope, and function within the poems of which they are a part, but similar in the terms of their basic construction.

In its use of a generalized fiction, *Ane Satyre of the Thrie Estaitis* shows the same characteristics. Langland uses Mede as the major term; Lindsay centers his play around Sensuality. As Langland shifts to the problem of the practical reform of society and the problem of just "mede" in the half-acre episode, so Lindsay shifts the second part of his play to the practical reform of society's sensuality. Like the second allegory in *Mum and the Soothsayer*, the first half of Lindsay's allegory uses the ridicule of Wisdom (Gude-Counsall) and his banishment as a generalization for evil rule, and the literal descent of God's avenger as a generalization for the punishment of irresponsible government. All these are examples of literal allegory. Lindsay's greater use of typical characters in the second half of the play implies, again, not a difference in kind but in degree of generalization. Both Veritie and Johne the Common-Weill, Sensualitie and Spiritualite are cast, not in the Palace of Fame or the Garden of Love, but in a generalized kingdom which represents no state of mind nor view of human nature, but a political state, and, specifically, the political state which is Scotland in 1552. The first half of the play relies more heavily on abstract presentation in its use of such characters as Sensualitie, Veritie, and Chastitie; the second half employs a more specific presentation through the use of characters such as Johne, the Pauper, and the Doctour of Divinitie. But both parts function in terms of the same view of the state in a fiction constructed in the same terms as the reality it represents: the kingdom.

We can see this fusion of representation and meaning more clearly, perhaps, if we turn to another allegory, *King Hart*. There the terms are the terms of kingship, but the meaning has nothing to do with kingship at all. The subject is the individual and his course through life, the same subject framed as a pilgrimage in Deguileville's poem, as a quest in the *Example of Virtue*. Yet King Hart rises, falls, and rises, again, just as Rex Humanitas goes through the same cycle. To classify the play and the poem together on this basis scarcely enlightens either and enlarges an apparent similarity of fiction to a principle of classification.[10] Both use the same fable, the career of a king, but the relation between fable and meaning sets them in very different groups indeed. *King Hart* is a metaphorical allegory: it discusses human life through a representation of kingship. *Ane Satyre of the Thrie Estaitis* is a literal allegory: it discusses the Scottish polity through a representation of political life or, in contemporary terms, it discusses Scottish kingship through a representation of Scottish kingship.

Yet, although one must first isolate and define the meaning of a text before evaluating its character as allegory, artistic value extends beyond the relative importance of the theme or the acumen with which it is analyzed. There is more to allegory than that: the fable itself must be artfully invented to best express the theme. *The Complaint of Scotland*, written in 1548, provides us with an analogue as close to the meaning of the *Thrie Estaitis* as one is likely to find in literary history. Responding to the same events, lashing out against the same excess in national and religious affairs that Lindsay found so repugnant, the anonymous author of the *Complaint* has nevertheless written a very different sort of allegory.[11] Like Lindsay, he too represents the three estates and discusses their social failings through dialogue. But his handling is much more facile, much less imaginative. He simply invents an entity named Dame Scotia, representative of the entire Scottish nation, and endows her with three sons, Clergy, Commons, Nobility. The result is hardly a dialogue, an interchange, but a debate, a long series of set speeches, with Dame Scotia acting as moderator and rebuking each speaker in turn. This debate may be compared with the second half of the *Thrie Estaitis* where the same criticisms form the basic material of the play.[12] Lindsay, too, invents a situation to detail the Scottish excesses, but this is a dialogue peopled with much more individualized characters: Johne, Pauper, the Doctour, Common Thift, and the exaggerated, acerbic Spiritualitie with his train of Parsone and Nune. And around these characters, the dramatist builds the attack of the rebellious upstart, Johne, who even as he complains in truth risks the charge of heresy as payment for his pains. Lindsay's is, of course, a more dramatic situation: it is a drama; it was meant to be played, not read. But for all the difference between the allegory as narrative and the allegory as drama, one may still say that *Ane Satyre of the Thrie Estaitis* is a more imaginative allegory, a better artwork than its cohort in Scottish politics, the *Complaint of Scotland*.

This is not to say that set speeches, in and of themselves, are artistically bad. On the contrary, they are an integral practice in allegorical literature. Lindsay's Gude-Counsall speaks the substance of the play's theme in his long speeches; Holicherche enunciates the principles in *Piers Plowman*.[13] But, in both cases, theory is enlivened by action. The principles are enlarged by action which both demonstrates and makes more specific the themes it illustrates. In the *Complaint of Scotland*, however, the long speeches are both the sum and substance of the allegory; they lack the variations of character and action which Lindsay so happily provides in the *Thrie Estaitis*.

But we begin to verge now toward questions of form and aesthetic judgment which may be more fruitfully considered in the last chapter where we will set the *Thrie Estaitis* among its peers, the "moralities" or, as we might rather call them, the dramatic allegories. This has been a descriptive chapter, constructed, not to form principles for the evaluation of all allegory, but to explore a few allegorical texts from the late Middle Ages. Because we have discussed none of them in detail, our observations can hardly be called complete. We have simply looked at those general characteristics and practices which illumine the nature of Lindsay's play.

From that examination, we have derived some knowledge about the range and variety encompassed in that monolithic term *allegory*. Beginning with those poems C. S. Lewis described as "homiletic," we saw that the topic of an individual allegory could be a description of human life as a series of encounters with evil *(Pilgrimage)*, an explication of knowledge itself *(Court of Sapience)*, or perhaps, a playful *jeu d'esprit* on the nature of love *(Court of Venus)*. Looking at the characters peopling the poems, we found that the emphasis lay, not in the change and development of character, but in the depiction and exposition of theme as action. Nor was this action arranged *serially* on the basis of realistic probability. Arranged episodically, the action functions, not in terms of the representation of character, but in terms of the developing argument, the representation of theme. Given this focus on the analysis of ideas, time and place are not relevant entities, and their influence, when relevant, is only suggested. The nature, causes, and consequences of the idea or ideas discussed are the focus of interest.

Next, narrowing our scope to those poems which specifically consider political questions, we saw that, given comparable material, specific writers produced wide variation in treatment or fable. Here, the texts appeared to fall into two general classes: the metaphorical and the literal allegory. Yet, even on the basis of this general description of structure, the simple characterization of the fiction was not enough. Both *Mum and the Soothsayer* and *Vox Clamantis* contain beast fables, metaphorical allegories, but the character and function of these fables within the larger context of the poems they ornament is quite different in concept and in function. The first vision of *Piers Plowman*, the first half of the *Thrie Estaitis*, and *King Hart* all employ the fiction of a king, but the last allegory is not about kingship at all, although, on the surface, it seems much closer to the play than the play does to *Piers*. Obviously, one must consider both the character of the fable and its relation to the ideas it encompasses before one can distinguish between apparently similar or dissimilar allegories. As medieval writers continually tell us, we must break through the shell of allegory to see the kernel of meaning. Once we have managed that less-than-easy task, allegory, shell and kernel, emerges as a single fruit existing in many varieties. Some are dry, perhaps, but many bear the sweet taste of thought informed by art.

NOTES

1. In "Allegory as Interpretation," *New Literary History* 2 (1973): 301–17, Morton W. Bloomfield summarizes the various applications of the term *allegory* in modern scholarship. His article is an excellent guide to diversity, with a bibliography in footnotes. In chapter 6, I attempt to set my own viewpoint within a more general context, and the reader will find specific citations there.

2. *Critical Approaches to Medieval Literature, Selected Papers from the English Institute, 1958–1959*, ed. Dorothy Bethurum (New York: Columbia University Press, 1960) contains essays which form a useful introduction to the fourfold method of interpretation. Here, my use of the term *allegory* has no connection with the method of biblical exegesis. See my article, "The Anglo-Saxon Phoenix and Tradition," *Philological Quarterly* 43 (1964): 1–13, where I do indeed employ allegorical exegesis, but in a relevant context.

3. Except for historical accident, these narrative poems and the plays might be called by the same name. Both are allegories; both are moralities. Both are written in verse; both frequently deal with comparable topics, and both are didactic. The only important difference lies in their manner of presentation: one sort of allegory is a drama; another sort is a narrative.

4. I exclude here the *Vitae de Dowel, Dobet, and Dobest* which is, of course, cast in the pilgrimage convention, and, as such, might be compared with Deguileville. For my purposes, only the first two *Visios* are relevant.

5. These materials also form the basis for book 8 in Gower's *Confessio Amantis*. Hawes's *Pastime of Pleasure* incorporates this topic as well. (*The Example of Virtue*, a less sophisticated allegory, was selected instead of *Pastime of Pleasure* because it provides a simpler and sharper contrast to the *Pilgrimage*.)

6. See Richard Southern's *The Medieval Theatre in the Round*, and Anna Jean Mill's "Representations of Lyndsay's *Satyre*." Southern argues that the stream shown in the *Castle of Perseverance* drawing must have been a moat behind the audience. Johne the Common-Weill's entrance (ll. 2428–30) is accompanied by a stage direction, "Heir sall Iohne loup the stank [ditch] or els fall in it." Another scene, that between the sowtar's wife and the taylor's wife (ll. 1368–87) takes place "be the watter syde." Both scenes, then, imply the "ditch" was part of the playing field, at least in Lindsay's experience, or that he specifically wrote the play for the field at Cupar, where a small stream still flows along the edge of town to join the river Eden.

7. *The Complete Works of John Gower*, ed. George C. Macaulay, vol. 4 (Oxford: The Clarendon Press, 1902) (hereafter cited as Gower's *Works*). A useful

translation is Eric W. Stockton's *The Major Latin Works of John Gower* (Seattle: University of Washington Press, 1962). Stockton believes that book 1 of *Vox* is an "afterthought" and not an integral part of the poem (see Introduction, p. 12). In this, he emphasizes Macaulay's suggestion that it "has certainly something of the character of an insertion" (Gower's *Works*, 4:xxxii), an opinion Macaulay cautiously advanced on the basis of the Laud MS, one of the five then known. I believe an analysis of Gower's rhetoric would reveal a close connection between his subsequent "animalistic" imagery and the substance of book 1. Unfortunately, *Vox* remains virtually unexplored. See also John Hurt Fisher's *John Gower* (New York: New York University Press, 1964).

8. R. W. Frank, Jr., "The Art of Reading Medieval Personification Allegory," *ELH* 20 (1953): 237–50.

9. *Mum and the Soothsayer*, ed. Mabel Day and Robert Steele, Early English Text Society, 199 (London: Kegan Paul, Trench, Trubner and Co., 1936). The poem is also called *Richard the Redeless*, a name Skeat gave to the shorter MS whose text he published in his edition of *Piers Plowman*, 1:603–26.

10. Cf. Willard Farnham's description of the early drama in *The Medieval Heritage of Elizabethan Tragedy* (Berkeley: University of California Press, 1936).

11. *The Complaynt of Scotlande*, ed. James A. H. Murray, Early English Text Society, ex. ser. 17 (London: N. Trubner and Co., 1872). My comments here are restricted to the dialogue between Dame Scotia and her sons, the central presentation. Bibliographical evidence in the form of a large number of cancels suggests extensive revision of the original text, and the insertion of the pastoral scene as "filler." Until the character of the cancels is ascertained, complete discussion of the *Complaint* is necessarily based on questionable evidence.

12. Lindsay emphasizes the excesses of the clergy, pokes fun at the merchants, but scarcely tweaks the nobility. In contrast the author of the *Complaynt* emphasizes the excesses of the Assured Scots, the nobles whose sympathies lay with the English, while apparently dealing less harshly with the sins of the commons, and especially the sins of the clergy. On this last, however, one may reserve opinion, since many of the cancels seem to appear at places where the clergy is under discussion—the result of some sort of censorship?

13. See T. P. Dunning, *Piers Plowman: An Interpretation of the A-Text*, especially pp. 26–27.

Chapter 5

Drama

Finally, we may assemble the elements which characterize *Ane Satyre of the Thrie Estaitis* as drama. While they do not exhaust the questions one might ask of the play, the preceding chapters have moved from one point of view to another and produced resultant shifts in focus. We began with the basic question of dating which must precede any critical analysis of the play. With 1552 taken as the logical point in time, our discussion shifted to the perspective of a sympathetic observer of that first, ideal performance in Cupar, Fifeshire. We asked what political memories would characterize that audience or, to put the question another way, we asked what political attitudes and knowledge Lindsay could assume in his audience as he wrote his play. While our history provides no keys to characters or specific events, the play does reflect social issues in the Scotland of Lindsay's lifetime. Given that view of contemporary history, we then turned from the literal material of the play to an exploration of its terms, which we have called its theme. We found those terms revealed in the late medieval discussion of reason and sensuality, associated with justice and injustice in the king and his relations with the nation.

At this point the analysis moved into another realm. The first three chapters embody the attempt to simply discover what the play is about. Once that queston was answered, we moved from the *what* to the *how*. Since the play is allegorical drama, allegorical narrative provides a way to see those practices common to drama and narrative. In that chapter, the discussion proceeded, perhaps, in a series of negatives, for many of the modern expectations, derived primarily from mimetic art, do not seem relevant. Time, place, characterization, organization of action, all are unlike the stories, the plays that usually form our basic knowledge of literary convention. Yet, once these differences are recognized, the reader no longer tries to force allegory into a realistic mold with which it shares only a surface resemblance. Then, one sees that characters are counters, terms in a developing argument. The quality and behavior of allegorical characters are based, not on psychological or realistic causation, but on the exposition of the argument's parts. At its best, the result is a stylized work of art where the characteristics of exposition and fiction merge to convey a didactic point of view designed to both teach and delight the sophisticated reader. In terms of analytic distinctions, then, we have arrived at the final stage of our exploration. Working now with the knowledge of relevant political history, literary history, and the allegorical mode, I will next view *Ane Satyre of the Thrie Estaitis* as drama.

We begin by setting *Ane Satyre* within a context of three other plays, selected for their surface similarities: Skelton's *Magnificence* (1516?), John Bale's *King Johan* (in its final revision, 1560), and *Respublica*, apparently written for Christmas presentation at Queen Mary's court in 1553.[1] We shall take the texts as "given"; that is, we shall not emphasize external factors such as the conditions of staging or the number of players available. That exclusion is not made to minimize the importance of such questions—indeed the most exciting recent publications on the morality play have come from just such concerns—but to narrow the area of inquiry. We know, for example, that the *Thrie Estaitis*, with its dining intermission, was a day-long performance presented outdoors on a playing field. With its separate *sedes* or acting locales, this "theater" provided a flexibility in the movement of actors and action that implies a relative ease in the management of exits and entrances.[2] The other three productions seem to be written for a fixed stage—certainly so in the case of *Respublica*, acted during the winter, and probably so for *King Johan* with its complex pattern of doubling. More important, perhaps, is the length of performance: Lindsay's play, in two parts (a total of 4,630 lines) is twice as long as *Respublica* (1,937 lines), and considerably longer than Bale's 2,721 lines or Skelton's 2,567 lines. (However, part 1 of the *Thrie Estaitis* is 2, 250 lines; part 2, 180 lines. Each part, then, is comparable in length to the other plays.) Obviously, Lindsay's contemporaries chose to, or were obliged to, work within a smaller compass.

Given these differences in theatrical production and length, we can see similarities and differences in the solutions which each writer invented within the confines of such external requirements. The most obvious similarity is their subject matter: all four plays are generally described as political moralities; two are Reformation polemics, one attacks the reformers; all four include royal characters and depictions of the governing classes; three are representations of historical events. All, in varying degrees, "saie not, as by plaine storye, / but as yt were in figure by allegory." [3]

But such similarities are essentially superficial, for differences are readily apparent. Perhaps the clearest contrast lies between *Ane Satyre* and *King Johan*, on the one hand, and *Magnificence*, on the other. If we are to call *Magnificence* a political play at all, it does not exist in the same spectrum with the others. Perhaps because it has had particular attention, Skelton's play has been subject to a series of confusing interpretations springing from the assertions of R. L. Ramsay, editor of the EETS text, who described the play as a personal satire directed against Cardinal Wolsey and Henry VIII. Since Skelton had been Henry's tutor, had written a *speculum principis*, and later produced narrative satire against Wolsey, Ramsay's identification of the play met with almost universal scholarly acceptance. A. R. Heiserman's essay on the play shook the foundations of that hypothesis, while W. O. Harris's independent study demolished the interpretation and brought the play into clear focus as a treatment of the theme of fortitude.[4] Harris traces the continued association of that virtue with royalty in an impressive examination of the treatises on kingship, and Heiserman, while he examines the rulers in such nonpolitical plays as *Nature* and the *Castle of Perseverance*, rightly compares the vaunting speeches of Magnificence with those of tyrants like Herod and Pharaoh in the medieval cycles. From this, he concludes that the play depicts the transformation of a king into an anti-king or tyrant and his subsequent reformation. In the face of such thorough studies, it is difficult to disagree, although one must suppress the urge to wonder how the fragment, *The Pride of Life*, and a poem like *King Hart*, compare with *Magnificence*. All three are about kings who indulge their folly and learn a hard lesson, yet in two of them the king is simply an allegorical figure which represents man in a particular guise. One wonders if the same may not be true for *Magnificence*.

Yet, it is not the function of this chapter to propose another interpretation for *Magnificence* (such an interpretation would have to examine the treatment of fortitude in general to see if it were capable of extension to other groups, or indeed, simply to that class which Sir Thomas Elyot called "governors," those who held high position but were not necessarily kings). If we grant that this is a play about a king, we can see at once that *Magnificence* is a play about the personal fortunes of that king. In terms of his royal function as ruler of the state, we see him perform only one sort of judicial act: the discharge and appointment of ministers. Moreover, these are ministers who have power over only two entities: the activities of Liberty and Largess, the king's actions and his purse. Thus, we never hear of the state of the realm, and, indeed, when Magnificence is struck by Adversity and Poverty, these events are presented in personal terms, not in terms of the king's deposition or potential conquest by a political enemy. Yet, how can a king lose his power and his palace otherwise?

In contrast, the *Thrie Estaitis* is much more particularized. We do indeed have a king's personal fortunes, but, from the beginning, the king is depicted as the giver of law and justice. We have already noticed how quickly the play moves, after the opening scenes of the king's entrapment, to a demonstration of the effect on the kingdom. The first part closes with the arrival of Correctioun, who not only reforms the king but calls for a parliament, a legal procedure to set the realm in order. We may see, then, that the literal action of *Magnificence* is roughly equivalent to the first scenes of Lindsay's play, but that Lindsay has compressed the process of personal decadence and reform. Skelton chose to concentrate on the king's personal fortune to the exclusion of a political emphasis, if we understand "political" to mean the relationship between the king and his realm. Skelton was writing a play about Fortitude and its place in the life of a man; Lindsay wrote a play about Sensuality as it affects a realm through the decadence of the king.

Politics are also central to *King Johan* where the issue is the king's right to rule the clergy, free from the "usurpation" of papal authority. Here, the king is virtuous and untempted but he is overwhelmed by superior forces. We see the effect of John's struggle on clergy, nobility, commons, and the state itself, allegorized as the Widow England. Again, in *Respublica*, the royal figure's personal fortunes are kept in the background, while the emphasis rests on the complaint of People, the object of the vice-ministers' depredations. The action is finally resolved, again in a legal setting, in a court, where the Four Daughters of God act as judges. *Ane Satyre, King Johan, Respublica*: these three are political plays because they deal with political issues. *Magnificence*, for all its royalty, only portrays the king as an individual human being.

But we may make further distinctions beyond this. In each of our three political plays, the historical reference is clear. As we have seen, Lindsay specifically refers to the state of Scotland, and, indeed, includes specific discussion of events in the final speech of Folly: we are given enough to know the general area of reference. Bale chooses to describe, allegorically, the literal events of King John's reign, as he interprets them, and ends his play with a generalized interpretation of the Reformation in England. The Prologue of *Respublica* specifically names Queen Mary as the Nemesis called up at the end (line 53) and, dated precisely in 1553, the text specifically refers to "these five yeres past" (line 1775) as the time span of the vices' activity, thus making the dramatic action equivalent to the reign of the reformers under Edward VI. All three plays, then, are representations of historical events, a representation that is clearly understood, although it is told "in figure by allegory," because the playwright has included the specific references which enable us to understand it in such terms. Thus, the three plays are clearly political, clearly geared to history although they speak in generalization; the fourth, *Magnificence*, while it includes some of the same terms, uses its opportunities for summary at the beginning and at the end to point to a set of attitudes about the human condition, especially as it exists "nowadays." Skelton does not discuss here the political nature of England.

Once, however, we see that *Respublica*, *King Johan*, and the *Thrie Estaitis* are allegorical representations of particular historical events, we should also see that they proceed in different terms. Lindsay's selection of sensuality as the cause for the social disorder is only one among many analyses he might have presented, if he chose and if he saw the nation in another fashion. (He might, for example, have used his *Tragedy of the Cardinal* as the basis for a play on the recent history of Scotland.) In contrast, Bale defends the Reformation and attacks the papacy by presenting a concept of sedition which argues for the necessity of the supreme power of the king over church and state. This argument derives from the reputed practices of the Roman church and demonstrates the inevitable tendency toward sedition locked within the very nature of that church. Bale's dramatic materials, then, are so ordered to produce such a conclusion. In *Respublica*, the theme is avarice, taken as the motivating factor during the reign of Edward VI when unscrupulous ministers gained power and advantage over the helpless state and protesting people.

Certainly, these thematic differences are fairly evident, but it is, of course, the dramatization which makes the plays distinguishable artistic entities. Of the three, *Respublica* is probably the easiest to discuss because it is closest, in structure, to later drama. In the manuscript, *Respublica* is divided into five acts, and the episodes are clearly organized into a single line of action within a five-act sequence. Within that action the emphasis or representation is consistently maintained on the vices: Avarice (alias, Policy), the old man who is leader and father to his three companions, Adulation (Honestie), Oppression (Reformation), and Insolence (Authoritee). The structure is simplicity itself. Act 1 provides us with the exposition of the vices' character and their plot; act 2 demonstrates their successful acquisition of power; act 3 demonstrates their exercise of the power. In act 3, the dramatist introduces the materials which will provide the conclusion of the play. He includes a scene in which People is introduced, providing the motivation for Respublica's later suspicions and for the confrontation of act 4. (In terms of the representation of England during the reformers' reign, the character implies that the people did not approve of the reign which preceded Queen Mary's.) He further invents, for act 3, a brief description of Verity (lines 907–14) which prepares the audience for her appearance in act 5. In act 4, Respublica gives People a full hearing which provides the first block to the power of the vices, and in the final act, the vices are apprehended and judged by the Four Daughters of God, with Truth (i.e. Verity) arriving first, followed by Mercy, Justice, and Peace.

Certainly, this is a clear and charming play. It uses only eleven characters, in three distinct groups: the Vices, the Virtues and Nemesis, and Respublica and People, the "innocent victims." One would think it almost a prototype for a psychomachia, especially since the roles of Respublica and People are so minor. But if we approach it from its past, we must call it rather poor allegory, for the terms break down in the final act. Why, we may ask, is the play resolved through the device of the Four Daughters of God. We might answer that this is simply a representation of the ordered realm in terms of the civic virtues. Such an answer seems to be an adequate allegorical interpretation, but the translation of the traditional dialogue in heaven over the fate of sinful man into a representation of the judgment of vices seems less adequate. Mercy's plea for the four *vices* seems strange, in a virtue, and the pardon and reformation of Adulation seems incredible when one considers the long history of the moral excoriation of flattery. In all honesty, Adulation pledges to "serve god and the Commonweale" (line 1891). Avarice is simply "pressed, as men doo presse a spounge" (line 1903), and the punishment of Oppression and Insolence is not represented, but deferred until a later date. In comparison to earlier vices who are executed on stage, hide in odd corners out of sight, or slip out of the country, this is odd treatment indeed. The explanation, however, is not hard to find. *Respublica* is Christmas entertainment: the vices are the central emphasis of the play, and their characters often lapse into charm, particularly in the case of Adulation whose flattery is of a particularly ingenuous sort. Thus, in a good-humored ending, the amusing villains are let off through a piece of pageantry which hardly uses the Four Daughters of God to serious effect. One cannot say much for the play as allegory; its terms are rather overwhelmed by delight in the characters.

But if *Respublica* is a lighter play than Lindsay's, we might turn to *King Johan* for a contrast at the other extreme. Bale's is not a charming play; it is a deadly serious dramatic argument cast in an interesting mixture of terms.[5] Although both Lindsay and Bale wrote Reformation plays, *King Johan* is certainly the more radical of the two. Lindsay's play criticizes clerical abuses, but it simply assumes the king's power to reform the clergy. It neither argues the relationship between papal and royal power, nor does it engage in doctrinal polemic, aside from its support of the vernacular for services and the translated Bible for the people. Whatever Lindsay's opinions were in private, his play is surprisingly moderate in its stress on the practical reform of clerical mores and in its silence on genuinely controversial issues like papal power and transubstantiation. (Indeed, it scarcely moves beyond the decrees of the latest provincial council in Scotland.) In contrast, Bale goes to the heart of the issue in his denunciation of papal authority and, using devices comparable to Lindsay's, presses them home to mortal ridicule. Like the *Thrie Estaitis, King Johan* is divided into two parts.[6] It begins, however. with an episode involving a citizen's complaint at court, the device which forms the second half of the *Thrie Estaitis.* Its king is a just ruler who immediately tries to remedy the complaint. Lindsay's play deals with internal politics; Bale's is a problem in external policy.

Beyond these matters of subject and definition, however, the mixture of historical and abstract treatment in *King Johan* provides effects which neither history nor allegory could achieve alone. Each of the parts may be divided into three episodes[7] with each triad marked by a summary at the end. These summaries, which end part 1 and part 2, point out and clarify the unity of the play. The play begins with the episode of Widow England's complaint to King John. This action is followed by the Parliament scene in which Nobility, Civil Order (a lawyer), and Clergy ostensibly agree to John's reforms. The third episode occurs in Rome at the papal court[8] and is broken momentarily by the exit of the vices and their reentry in clerical garb. In this last episode of part 1, the plot against John is created. Next the Interpreter appears and, in thirty-five lines, summarizes and comments upon the action, bridging the action of the first part with the second, and including in his summary the final episode which he describes as the reforming acts of "our late kynge Henrye." Part 2 then begins with a brief episode which shows Stephen Langton (Sedition's new name) marshaling support among the three estates of England; a longer episode follows which includes John's acquiescence and death. Then, the text suggests, the play immediately turns into the third episode, the sequence with Verity and Imperial Majesty, which returns to allegorical statement. The action ends with a series of speeches by Nobility, Clergy, and Civil Order, in which the play is again summarized, commented upon, and ended with praise of Queen Elizabeth, the latest in the line of godly rulers.[9]

Now, looking back over the total structure of the play, we can see that it begins in abstract statement, breaks near the end of the first part into historical statement[10] which continues through the second part and includes the death of John. At this point the play returns to abstraction, without a break, using once again the figure of Sedition and introducing the new characters of Verity and Imperial Majesty, the successful reformer who represents Henry VIII.

While this pattern of allegory-history-allegory has confused some readers, it seems evident that such a strategy enables Bale to dramatize the generalization he provides for us in the two summaries. We are to see past and present as one continuum with the same forces operating in English history despite the separation of time. Sedition is the method and aim of the Papists; thus we see the principle in operation as an abstraction and we see the abstraction operating in the specific historical personage. Stephen Langton is simply the thirteenth-century manifestation of Sedition; his historic superior, the pope (in that case Innocent III), is simply the thirteenth-century embodiment of Usurped Power; Swynset is Dissimulation, the pseudo martyr the nefarious clergy encourages and canonizes. The identification between the abstraction and the living person is pushed back in time by a reference to Henry II and Thomas á Becket,[11] pushed forward in time by the final sequence representing the recent successful English Reformation which is still threatened by events in Elizabeth's reign. As the episodes are performed before our eyes, the principal and the particular merge to give us a double vision of the reality which sees the same forces operating across the centuries.[12]

We can see Lindsay operating in a comparable fashion, but his is a play, not between abstract and historical figures or terms, but between abstract and typical figures, arranged in a different pattern and operating, not by merging the two, not by *identification*, but by association. As such, it appears less confusing, more conventional than Bale's method.[13] Yet, the *Thrie Estaitis* are organized in a comparable sequence of three episodes to each part.[14] In part 1, the temptation and fall of Rex Humanitas provides one episode which includes the arrival of Sensualitie and the introduction of the trio of vices—Flatterie, Falset, and Dissait. The second episode begins with the introduction of Veritie and continues through the Sowtar-Taylor scene to end in Chastitie's imprisonment. The third episode includes the arrival and preliminary reformation by King Correctioun. If we look at this division in terms of function, we can see that the first episode, in dramatizing the king's slide into sin, demonstrates the causes for social disruption. The second episode, with its mistreatment of Veritie and Chastitie, shows the actual social effects of such disorder, and the third episode introduces the factor, God's correction, which produces the reformation of the realm.[15]

Such division seems to hold true for part 2 as well. There, the action resumes with the Pauper's episode. A much longer block of action follows: the Parliament episode, which ends with the reading of the laws. The third segment one might call the finale: this includes the hanging scene and the sequence with the clown, Folly, which ends the play. Analyzing, again, in terms of function, we can see that only the Parliament episode is an integral, a necessary part of the plot. As such, it is really an extension of the action begun in the King Correctioun episode of part 1: the enactment of reform. The Parliament episode consists of two parts. In the first, a sequence of complaints is quickly turned from general charges by Temporalitie's immediate agreement to reform the secular governing class (see lines 2705–37). The episode then moves into the second part with its examination of the excesses of the spiritual estate. This second sequence contains the examination of the clergy and includes the Doctour's sermon and the subsequent, literal unfrocking of priest and nun. Thus the Parliament episode consists essentially of two sorts of action: the complaint and the clergy's examination. In terms of the story itself, only the Parliament scene adds essential action by completing the reformation begun by King Correctioun in part 1. The other episodes of part 2 perform different functions.

We have seen earlier how the Pauper episode serves to summarize and restate the issues raised in part 1.[16] It does so through two "beats" of action: the scene with Diligence in which lay injustices are exposed by Pauper's example and the subsequent action in which the Pardoner exemplifies clerical abuses. Comparably, the final episode is essentially one of summary. In the hanging sequence, each of the long speeches serves the purpose of general satire. Theft ironically attacks thieves and criminals, Dissait summarizes the vices of the merchants, Falset details the failings of the craftsmen, while the capping and final speech is, suitably, an attack on the friars delivered by the play's major vice, Flatterie. Taken together, all of these speeches summarize the faults and the complaints which have formed the substance of the play: the decadent state of a society in need of moral reformation. The second round of summary begins on another plane which, at the level of literal action, seems totally unconnected with events in the play. (Compare the surprising and, at first, seemingly irrelevant introduction of Pauper.) Just as the play seems to be over, Folly enters in a scene that begins in sheer nonsense—now the fool, too, makes his complaint about the realm. The bad manners of the sow at Schogait become a comic parody of the complaints in Parliament, presented earlier, and, in a touch of irreverence which twits the Doctour's sermon, the fool ascends the pulpit and invites everyone to buy his folly hats. Uproariously, the play ends on the delightful note of the author mocking his own major scene: the complaint and examination of Parliament. But the Folly scene is more than that, of course. It joins the preceding scene of the Vices' farewell to form an episode of summary. Although the play speaks in general, although the vices in their last speeches direct the audience's attention to general follies, Folly himself speaks in plain English and shoots his darts at specific

examples of specific failings in the contemporary world.[17] The play
ends, then, in a satiric bombardment and turns the audience toward
current politics with a final scene designed to recall, by parody, the
most important episode of the play, the episode which proposes
specific measures applicable to Scottish politics. While the essential
action of the play ends with the reading by Diligence of the laws, the
final episode provides the amusing summary which drives the
author's points home while it ends the play in ironic laughter.

We can see, then, that *Ane Satyre of the Thrie Estaitis*, like Bale's *King
Johan*, is a single play divided into two parts, each containing three
episodes. Both playwrights use the first half of the play for exposition
of the situation, briefly introducing the elements which will form the
second part of the play. In that second part, the major portion of the
action is devoted to the resolution of the problem presented in part 1.
In a final episode, however, the author provides a summary which
sharpens and repeats the themes of the play in terms of current
politics. Similarly, the two playwrights mix generalized and particularized statement in their selection and use of characters.

But these resemblances are similarities in general approach and
method. Within those confines, the two plays diverge in the use of
particular devices and, as a result, in the effects their plays produce.
We have already suggested that, in his selection and use of character,
Bale constructs an *identification* between his historical characters and
the vices they embody, a method which suggests he has turned the
vices' traditional change of name to another, more immediate use.
Lindsay, on the other hand, proceeds by *association*. With the virtues
and vices set up in the first part of the play, he shifts his terms to
another set of typical characters who are closer to literal, direct statement but who do not have the specific historical reference of a King
John and his fellows. Yet Lindsay does not drop the first set of terms.
In part 2, he intensifies his emphasis by presenting a new group of
characters who share the functions of the first group by association.
These typical characters perform most of the action but are periodically advised or helped by the first group of characters, who, for the
most part, remain on stage throughout. Thus, in part 2, we have the
vices entering for the Parliament along with the estates to which they
are linked in their final speeches in part 1 and part 2. We see Veritie
and Chastitie entering into the complaint sequence with Johne the
Common-Weill and Pauper, while Sowtar and Taylor are used as
evidence against the clergy. We see Sensualitie and Flatterie (who is

dressed as a friar during most of the action) associated briefly during part 1 with the clergy, participating on the side of the clergy in part 2.

The basic situation the two authors have chosen to dramatize is also quite different. Bale's king is a virtuous man who is subverted by external powers and whose struggle occupies most of the play. On the other hand, Lindsay's dramatization of a humanly sinful king is simply one part of a dramatic process which moves beyond the king's fate as the action progresses. Yet Bale, no less than Lindsay, uses his king as a vehicle for the theme of the king's rightful power over the clergy. Given the view of history implied in *King Johan* as a series of events, separated by time, but united by principles of action and behavior, the final episode of a king succeeding where John had failed is linked by theme as well as by the characters carried over from the immediately preceding action. Like Bale, Lindsay links his final episode of summary through its theme, but the Scottish dramatist connects it by unification of action as well. The hanging of the vices is not necessary to the representation. It might have been done in a brief pantomime, simply reported on stage, or completely omitted: the play would be no less comprehensible without it. But, functioning as summary, the scene is also a natural extension of the vices' imprisonment in the preceding episode. In contrast, Folly's scene has no such causative connection; it is simply an extraneous scene in terms of the major action, introduced for the sake of ending the play with entertainment and more specific satire. Lindsay connects it, however, by creating it as a parody of the Parliament episode which formed the actual end of the necessary action, and, indeed, he parodies both parts of that central episode in the mock complaint and the mock sermon which parallels the sermon of the examination scene.

Nevertheless, Bale's play has the appearance of greater unity simply because the causal relationships between episodes are clearer to our modern eyes: the interest of the action focuses around King John and that focus of a single story is maintained until the final episode. At best, that last action seems an unintegrated epilogue, or at worst, irrelevant, until one sees the play from the viewpoint of thematic analysis. Bale narrows his theme to one man's history and uses that history as the example of his generalization. In this, his play is like *Magnificence* with its account of one man's fortune. The difference between *King Johan* and *Magnificence*, however, lies in Bale's clearly political theme, and in his representation of a historical point of view which merges the abstract and the particular, the historic and the

"modern." In comparison to *King Johan*, Lindsay's play appears fragmented in terms of its action until one sees the theme developing
through the representation of different social groups and varying
tendencies abroad in the nation. Unlike either Skelton or Bale, Lindsay expands his theme to a detailed representation of the nation,
inventing episodes to show the extent and effect of Sensualitie's influence on the rest of the country. As a result, the *Thrie Estaitis* is more
dependent upon a perception of thematic unity than either *King
Johan* or *Magnificence*.

In terms of structural pattern, the three plays show several basic
similarities and differences. *King Johan* and the *Thrie Estaitis* reveal
more similarities with each other than either does with *Respublica*.
Both Reformation plays use a two-part structure; both consist of three
episodes within each part. In both, action introduced in part 1 is
completed in part 2; both implement their essential action with
episodes designed to function as summary. Yet, within their comparable framework, the two writers select different modes of statement.
Bale moves from an emphasis on abstract character to historical
character and back to abstract again. In contrast, Lindsay moves from
an emphasis on abstract character in part 1 to the use of typical
characters in part 2. Thus, the dramatists' handling of characters as
terms in a developing theme or argument differs. On the other hand,
Respublica is structurally quite distinct from both *King Johan* and the
Thrie Estaitis. Here, the action itself is unified and the number of
characters is significantly reduced. The play is shorter (1,937 lines to
Lindsay's 4,630 lines). The characters continue throughout the play
as the single set of terms in which the theme and the action are
presented. Indeed, *Respublica* is very like a post-Shakespearean
drama. Yet, while *Respublica* is generally regarded as a single action
(and, in terms of action, it is), it suffers from thematic flaws. Its very
failings, from the thematic view, provide a measure which sets *Ane
Satyre of the Thrie Estaitis* midway between the comedy of *Respublica*
and the savage satire of *King Johan*.

I have said that the play breaks down in the final act because the
use of the Four Daughters of God, is, in terms of allegory, utterly
inappropriate for judging and disposing of the vices. But we may go
further and question the validity of the author's entire conception, *in
the context of an anti-Reformation play*. Certainly, this loads the terms
against *Respublica*, but the basic confusion of the play lies in the use of
the vices who are apparently designed to ridicule the reformers, just

as Lindsay's vices are designed to ridicule the conservative faction in the church. The vices of *Respublica* are simply too charming for the thematic meaning which their names and a good part of their dialogue implies. The problem is, in small, a little like the problem Jonson faced in *Volpone*. What does one do with villains who become delightful?

Now, both Skelton and Lindsay depict their villains in a manner which limits their humor. In *Magnificence*, Skelton limits the kinds of action he permits his vices to enact on stage. While his long monologues require clever actors to hold audience interest, the alternative—presenting the materials of the monologues in terms of action—would expand the role of the vices and distort the emphasis of the play. As it is, he devotes 971 lines (lines 403–1374) to the representation of the vices with long individual speeches which carefully describe their characteristics. At the same time, he breaks up this exposition by alternating monologue with dialogue, including, as a final piece of liveliness, the sequence where Fancy and Folly exchange the owl and the mangy dog. While the mock quarrel between Courtly Abusion and Cloked Collusion as upstarts who argue over precedence and court fashion and the wildly foolish exchange of animals by Fancy and Folly *is* amusing, we tend to laugh superior laughter at the perpetrators of jokes. Skelton ends the sequence with Crafty Conveyance's monologue which once again reminds us of the serious threat posed by the vices. Beyond this careful exposition of their natures, we see the vices only three times more and in separate groups. Courtly Abusion and Cloked Collusion appear in a scene with Magnificence, feigning to ask his favor for Measure; Folly and Fancy appear to mark the king's downfall; and, finally, Crafty Conveyance, Cloked Collusion, and Conterfeit Countenance appear briefly, near the end, where they mock Magnificence, as they move on to celebrate with a night at the stews. In all three scenes, the vices are associated with a disaster that is enacted on stage: the cruel treatment of Measure, the king's shock at his loss of station, and the point at which Magnificence lies helpless, just before Despair and Mischief enter with their terrible suggestions of suicide.

Skelton, then, repeatedly presents the vices in association with action demonstrating the serious effects of their influence. Before they are introduced, he begins the play with a scene which provides the background for our view of the vices: Felicity's opening speech discussing the dangers of rash action, and the ensuing debate with

Liberty when the necessity of rule by Measure is asserted. Since we know what the terms and the stakes are, we understand the nature of the threat the vices represent, and we see the effects of that threat associated with disaster in the second half.

In contrast, *Respublica* presents the vices in a much more direct fashion. The play begins with a monologue by Avarice. It is an amusing speech in which Avarice takes the audience into his confidence as friends. Here, Avarice describes his love of money, in realistic fashion, as a necessity: "Full lytle knowe men the greate nede that I am yn, / doo not I spende dailie of that that I doo wynne? / then age cometh on and what ys a lytle golde / to kepe a man by drede that is feble and olde?" (lines 111–14). It is hard to blame a man too much for hoarding money in fear of age and need. The problem here is that we are met with too much characterization. One can disapprove of an insolent, braggart vice who vaunts his illegal deeds; it is more difficult to disapprove of a mealy mouthed old man, anxious to court response and approval. Matters are hardly helped when the vices are joined by Adulation; the boy uses delightfully exaggerated, utterly transparent flattery: "Oh noble Insolence, if I coulde singe as well / I wolde looke in Heaven emonge Angells to dwell" (lines 123–24). Such flattery does not seem threatening; it seems endearingly naïve, and, delivered by a boy actor, such an impression of the ingenuous might be intensified beyond the character of the lines themselves. These vices engage our sympathies, not our disdain.

But one would have to extensively analyze and compare the rhetoric of *Respublica* and *Magnificence* to do more than merely suggest this point. We may see the difference in treatment more quickly, perhaps, if we look at the treatment of Respublica herself and of People. Respublica is hardly characterized at all; she is simply a convenient queen, present in the play to provide the standard transfer of power to the vices, so that we may see, in act 3, the full extent of their capacity for rapine. But it is a capacity for rapine that we only hear about as we see them glorying in their bags of money and new possessions. Their actions in terms of on-stage demonstration of effect are only suggested by the soliloquies which characterize the queen as patient, hopeful, and responsible. In her first soliloquy (act 2, scene 1, lines 439–60), she sounds the *ubi sunt* theme and explains the relationship between the state of the realm and the nature of its governors: this is essentially a thematic soliloquy, for the vices then demonstrate how evil governors may gain control. But, thereafter, we find

Respublica's soliloquies expressive of her character. In act 3 (lines 588–609), she hopes that her ministers will recover her prosperity, and in act 4 (lines 969–84), she describes the uncertainty she feels at People's complaints. Beyond this anxious nattering, we see no evidence of change in her character or behavior; neither the irresponsible indulgence and failure of action Lindsay provides in Rex Humanitas nor, with Skelton, the lesson in court malice and the typically vaunting braggadocio of Magnificence, both of which stand for a state of moral decadence. Respublica is simply a nice lady who is wronged.

But even this might be no flaw in the play if it were not for the handling of a more important element: People, the character who provides the only evidence of the vices' rapacious activities. From People's first appearance, he is characterized as a clown, both a country bumpkin and a source of comedy. This effect is produced, in large part, by the language with which the author endows him: it is a broad Southern dialect, pushed to a comic extreme by the use of malapropisms and the exaggerated use of "proper" language:

> *People.* whares Rice puddingcake? I praie God she bee in heale.
> *Adul[ation].* who? Rice puddingcake?
> *peopl.* yea alese dicts commonweale.
> *Adul.* I knowe hir not.
> *peopl.* masse youe liest valeslye in your harte.
>   She is this waie. che wart, a false harlot youe arte.
> *Adul.* I knowe Respublica.
> *peopl.* yea, Marie, whare is shee?
> *Adul.* She is buisie nowe /
> *peopl.* Masse, ere iche goe, chill hir zee, for this waie she came.
> *Respub[lica].* lett my people come to mee.
> *Adulac.* God forbydde els. Come on, People, is this same shee?
> *People.* yea malkin ist.
> *Resp.* People, what wolde with me nowe?
> *Peopl.* Marye, mustres, madame, my ladie, howe doe youe?
>   (3. 3. 636–45)

It is the language of a peasant: innocent, clumsy, unconsciously comic in its attempt to use the "right" terms. Certainly, People is no threat to our clever vices, and, in his second appearance (4. 4), they easily

outtalk him and send him home, no worse, on stage, for the encounter. This final sally (lines 1142–65) might be staged as a physical
attack on People by the vices, but it is difficult to see how even a brief
beating could be anything but comic when People's final lines simply
convey an almost courteous resentment:

> *Avar.* It were best for youe, freend, all mourmouringe to cease.
> *People.* bum vei than, chil een goo home, and vaire holde mi peace.
> *Insol.* Dooe soo by my reade / & fall to honest laboure.
> *Avar.* hens home & bee quiete, and thow shalte fynde favour.
> *people.* Then chil byd youe vare well.
> *Oppr.* no woordes but hens a pace. this was doone as shoulde bee.
> *Avar.* this was doone in right place.
> *people.* but howe, one worde erche goe / yele geve volke leave to thinke?
> *Oppr.* No, marie, will we not, nor to looke but winke.
> *people.* yes, by gisse, but chil loe, naie loe thare, þought is free, and a catt
> þey zaith maie looke on a king pardee. *exeat.*
>
> (4. 4. 1156–66)

People, too, is a charming character, but his characteristics, coupled with the brevity of his appearances, destroy any serious effect he
might have had as a demonstration of the pernicious effect of the
vices. Since that effect is never really demonstrated—neither in the
character of Respublica nor in the presentation of the only
complainant—our delight in the vices' antics rules the performance:
we are amused to see the villains let off lightly in a final pageant which
simply ignores the serious doctrinal character of the Four Daughters
of God. Poor People is only an ineffective instrument for social complaint, and, it would seem, in terms of the play, that complaint is not
really the aim of *Respublica*: it simply goes through the motions, using
the anti-Reformation theme of avarice, not for serious point but to
provide a gay little entertainment for a holiday society which, apparently, holds itself secure from the threats of the former reign. It does
not divert one's attention from such serious issues by *not* presenting
them; it simply declines to take them seriously.

Yet, if one cannot justly complain of *Respublica*'s lack of moral
substance, one can see, by comparison, how Lindsay avoids such a
comic tone. In part 1, he shows us the moral decline of the king, but,
instead of resolving his action in a linear extension of the king's per-

sonal fortunes, as Skelton does, he uses his virtues, not as devices to resolve the vices' action, but as further demonstrations of the effects of Sensualitie and her attendant vices, Flatterie, Falset, and Dissait. Then, switching his terms to the particularity of typical figures, he introduces two characters to represent the common man's complaints: Pauper and Johne the Common-Weill. He has already injected rough, peasant humor into the play with Sowtar and Taylor. Like Veritie and Chastitie, the two craftsmen demonstrate the effects of the vices' behaviour, and like the virtues, they also join in the official complaint during the Parliament episode. But the thrust of the complaint belongs to Johne, aided by his auxiliary, Pauper.

By investing his low comedy in Sowtar and Taylor, Lindsay gains some of the comic effect provided by People in *Respublica*. At the same time, he avoids vulgarizing the complaint at court by giving that function to two characters, Johne and Pauper, who are not presented in terms of low comedy. He further engages our sympathies for these characters by making Pauper a poor man from Lothian, an area recently ravaged by the English and the French, who is hounded by an avaricious parish priest, denied justice at both "sessioun" and "seinʒe," and, finally, robbed of his last groat by the Pardoner's trick. Similarly, we see Johne bursting on the scene with blunt indignation and, like Veritie herself, threatened by the heresy accusation which puts him in real danger of death by fire. Certainly the seriousness of such events sharply contrasts with the treatment of People who is simply sent home by the vices. The confrontation between accuser and accused involves more serious consequences in *Ane Satyre of the Thrie Estaitis* than it does in *Respublica*. Unlike the latter, the Scottish play also enacts the punishment of the vices and their associates, the clergy. The clergy are stripped of their fraudulent religious garb and sent off to exile, while the vices, in a scene perhaps too realistic for our modern taste, are actually executed on stage. This is quite a contrast to the vices' punishment in *Respublica*.

But if the *Thrie Estaitis* is more serious than *Respublica*, *King Johan* shows us another extreme. Here is a play almost devoid of comedy and devoted to satire as bitter as Jonathan Swift's. Bale's play contains no peasant humor, no innocent, foolish characters. Even the scenes which provide a bit of horseplay carry their weight of didactic thrust: the scene between Dissimulation and Sedition at Rome (lines 620–758), and the pantomime of the piggyback ride provided by the vices (lines 779–58). The depiction of the clergy produces a major difference in effect between the *Satyre* and *King Johan*. On the surface, Lindsay's play is indeed a satire of the *three* estates: he criticizes the head of state in his portrayal of Rex Humanitas; he associates his vices with the nobility and the commons as well as with the clergy. But the reformation of the king and of Temporalitie occurs quickly and is represented, in both cases, by a simple avowal to reform, while the accusation and examination of the clergy is expanded to occupy most of the Parliament episode. Certainly, the clergy is attacked. But Lindsay blunts his satiric effect in the last episode by turning the audience's attention again to the general satire of all the classes contained in the vices' final speeches and to the comic entrance of Folly which follows. The latter plunges the play into wild nonsense, before the final attack on specific political events which ends the play. In effect, Lindsay expands his attack on the clergy, but he also surrounds it with other materials which soften the over-all effect of that attack. By contrast, Bale's play is a direct confrontation between king and clergy which relentlessly traces out the methods of the clergy, not simply in terms of their personal moral behavior or their failure to enlighten the people as preachers and moral exemplars. In Lindsay's account, the priests pervert the people (and thus the nation) largely by their example and their sins of omission. In *King Johan*, the clergy's corruption reaches out to destroy the state itself through the agency of illegal, external power. Lindsay's priests are Scotsmen; Bale's are wicked foreigners who bleed the nation for the benefit of Rome and Babylon.

The satiric difference is also evident in the playwright's use of religious parody. While Lindsay certainly uses such parody, it is lighter, less serious, than the parodies Bale works into the very structure of his plot, where crucial scenes in the developing action are clothed in the materials of the Roman liturgy. In the second part of *King Johan*, Sedition-Langton implements his plot against the king by using the confessional. The subversion of Nobility occurs in a parodied formula of confession which begins in the proper form:

nobelyte. benedicte
sedycyon. Dominus: In nomine domini pape amen:
         say forth yowr mynd in gods name.
nobelyte. I haue synnyd agaynst god; I knowledge my selfe to blame
    In the vij dedly synns, I haue offendyd sore
    gods ten commaundyments, I haue brokyn eu'more

my v. boddyly wyts, I haue on-godly kepte
the works of charyte, In maner I houe owt slepte.

(Ll. 1153–60)

The confessional scene is immediately followed by the subversion of
Clergy and Civil Order. This time, the device is a pardon "a pena et
culpa" which Sedition-Langton accompanies with a long catalogue of
"relics," ending with the blessing so often repeated in the play, "In
nomine domini pape amen" (lines 1119–1235). A confession is presented again, after John's acquiescence to the church and before his
murder. This time it is Dissimulation, in the guise of the Cistercian
Simon of Swynset, who reveals his poisoning scheme to Sedition and
receives absolution and the promise of perpetual masses for his soul
in return. The inference is clear, of course: the confessional is a place
for secret plotting against the state.

Bale incorporates two other uses of ritual into his presentation of
the clergy. The episode at Rome begins and ends with such a ritual.
At the end of the Parliament sequence, the stage is empty for a moment. Sedition appears, this time at Rome (as we see from his brief
speech when Dissimulation enters, and from subsequent speeches).
When Dissimulation enters, he sings a litany which ends with a brief,
garbled prayer and the chant, mocking the litany response: "A
Iohanne Rege iniquo, libera nos domine" (line 646). Later, Usurped
Power (the pope) and Private Wealth (Cardinal Pandulphus) enter
reciting a parody of the psalm in comparably broad Latin: "Super
flumina babilonis: suspendim[us] organa nostra / quomodo cantabim-
[us] canticum bonum, In terra aliena" (lines 759–60). The episode
ends, after the principals have changed into official robes, with the
pope performing the excommunication ritual, accompanied by Cardinal Pandulphus and Sedition, now presented as Langton. With bell,
book, and candle, the pope, whom we have just seen dressed as a
careless nobleman, exercises his awful power. Part 1 ends here, at the
point where this parody of religion would leave its full impact on the
audience, a point where, as the Interpreter emphasizes: "These
bloudsuppers thus, of cruelties and spyght / Subdues thys good
kynge, for executynge ryght" (lines 1088–89). While it is certainly not
objective truth, Bale presents the Roman Church through a devastat-
ing parody of religious ritual used for cynically evil ends. Litany,
confession, pardon, excommunication: all are performed by Sedition
and his *frères*, intertwining papistry with the murder of King John and
the destruction of English life.

By contrast, Lindsay's use of such elements seem moderate. His parody of relics, coupled with the illegal divorce of Sowtar and his wife, is put into the role of the Pardoner, that disreputable friar who had figured in literature for centuries. Although the Pardoner is certainly associated with the abuses of the clergy in the play, this is is a much less direct method than Bale's use of Sedition, a cardinal and powerful clergyman, as the agent of such acts. Beyond this, Lindsay uses only two other religious forms. The vices briefly parody baptism in their change of names (lines 779–800), but the parody consists of no more than an exchange of phrases in English: "Bot ȝit anis name the bairn[is] name. / Discretioun, Discretioun in God[i]s name." [18] The other parody briefly creates the atmosphere of a heresy trial when Spiritualitie sets Flatterie forth as the friar to act as inquisitor and prosecutor in Johne's examination. He addresses Johne in the outrageous fashion of the heresy trial accounts: "Fals huirsum carle schaw furth thy faith . . . Quhom in trowis thou, fals monster man-git?" (lines 2994–98).[19] Ending the recitation of his Creed in English before the crucial final part, Johne is prompted by Correctioun himself to continue, and ends with "I trow Sanctam Ecclesiasm, / Bot nocht in thir Bischops nor thir Friers / Quhilk will for purging of thir neirs, / Sard vp the ta raw and doun the vther. / The mekill Devill resaue the fidder" (lines 3024–28). This is, of course, a vulgar slap at the clergy's sexual immorality, but Lindsay stops the proceedings here with Correctioun's judgment that Johne is "ane gude Christian man" (line 3060), and the action moves on to other concerns. Having suggested the atmosphere of a heresy trial with all its associations of official injustice, Lindsay pursues the satire no further. His touch is light. The point is raised and the audience is left to make its response and draw its own conclusion.

Lindsay's heaviest use of religious parody is relegated to the traditional Pardoner, a disreputable figure at best. In his two other parodies, he simply suggests the ritual and eschews special vestments, crosses, bells, and the Latin texts he might have used. We do not miss such elements in Lindsay's representation, but a comparison with Bale's methods shows us that the Scottish reformer might have chosen comparable methods if a comparable degree of satire were his purpose. As a Reformation play, *Ane Satyre of the Thrie Estaitis* must be placed between *Respublica* and *King Johan*. More serious than the former, it nevertheless provides some of its easy comedy in its use of characters. Less ferocious than the latter, it nevertheless uses serious materials for satirical attack.

Looking at comparable morality plays, we can see that Lindsay's drama shares characteristics with *Magnificence, Respublica* and *King Johan*. Yet, despite their comparable cast of characters and their common concern with the fate of kings, these four plays demonstrate decided differences in handling. Essentially, I have analyzed them from two basic points of view: in terms of material, the subject and theme of each play; and in terms of method, the plot structure, the use of character, and the special devices used to create audience response. Through this analysis, we see *Ane Satyre of the Thrie Estaitis* as a political play constructed, like *King Johan*, in two parts which are held together by episodes designed to provide summary and restatement of theme. Differing from Bale in his choice and explanation of a political situation, Lindsay also manipulates his characters in a different way, inventing two sets of characters who are grouped together in terms of their *association* with reason or with sensuality. In contrast, Bale uses the traditional disguising of the vices to move from abstract to historical statement: Sedition becomes Stephen Langton; Dissimulation becomes Simon of Swynset. This characteristic we have called *identification* to distinguish it from Lindsay's use of character.

If the *Thrie Estaitis* is most like *King Johan* in its political emphasis and in its basic structure, its differences appear when we set it next to *Magnificence* and *Respublica*. The contrast in subject is immediately evident. *Magnificence*, a play about fortitude, concentrates on the personal fortune of one character, presented as a king. While Lindsay's fable (in the first part of the play) appears comparable to Skelton's, that appearance is essentially superficial, for Lindsay's portrayal concentrates on the king as the dispenser of justice. It is not the king's personal fate, but his relationship to the social health of the realm which constitutes Lindsay's invention of dramatic action. *Respublica*, on the other hand, rather ignores the question of kingship to concentrate instead on the exposition of the vices which lately infected the realm, all of which are centered on the desire for gain embodied in the central vice, Avarice.

Beyond these differences, *Respublica* also provides a contrast in dramatic effect. Although his subject is ostensibly serious, the creator of *Respublica* handles his materials in such a way that the play moves closer to lighthearted comedy than to serious political comment. The edge is taken off by the characterization of the vices; the treatment of the allegory is incongruous both in the portrayal of People, the complainant, and in the final judgment scene. This contrasts with

Skelton's handling of the vices, and with Lindsay's separation of his complainants from the appeals of low comedy. Yet, while Lindsay makes his points seriously, he does not use Bale's sharp weapons of relentless parody and pointed expansion and emphasis of clerical episodes. Surely, *King Johan* provides an instructive contrast in the range of Reformation satire. Taking that play as one extreme of satiric attack, we can see that the *Thrie Estaitis* is both adroit and temperate in its attack on "the abusions used in the country by diverse sorts of Estates."

If we may risk a final summing up, then, perhaps we may put our elements together with terms which may now take on new meaning. Sir David Lindsay's *Ane Satyre of the Thrie Estaitis* is a play produced in 1552 which portrays the general failure of civic and religious leadership in Scotland. It analyzes that failure and calls for the needed reform through the use of an allegory designed to demonstrate the effects of sensuality on the Scottish nation which, in following the sensual life, has eschewed verity and chastity, the qualities associated with the life of reason. This dramatic allegory, like others of its kind, is cast in the form of a literal—not a metaphorical—fable which quite simply does not observe the later literary canons of verisimilitude. On stage, it is presented in two parts (i.e., with an intermission) which form one whole. Its episodes are invented, ordered, and controlled to produce a temperate attack on the social evils of the time. This, then, is the generalized description of the play. Naturally, it is true only as far as the details of the argument presented in preceding chapters are true.

The development of this description has taken us into two areas which seem central to the understanding of the morality play. Quite simply, these are the areas of allegory and of didactic drama. In both topics, I have argued for an order based on the requirements of argument. Unlike an essay or an oration, however, the texts examined here proceed through the invention of a fiction or fable which is ordered to argue the individual thesis as the story develops. With such an emphasis, characters are of lesser importance, functioning as counters or terms in the argument which is embodied in the action and the dialogue. A particular feature of that dialogue is the use of long speeches which I have called thematic soliloquies. These speeches, again, serve the uses of the argument and usually function as exposition of the points in the argument or as summaries designed to make clear the development of the argument toward a conclusion.

Taking this position a further step, we might ask what differences exist between narrative and dramatic allegory. I think we should have to say "very little, except the obvious one." Narrative allegory is designed to be read—silently or aloud—by one person, with or without an audience of listeners. As such, its relative length is largely under the control of the writer who may make it as long or as short as his material or his inclination allows, just as the modern novelist may write a short or a long novel. Dramatic allegory is designed to be enacted, a fact that requires the author to work his commentary into the speeches of the various actors. He is further limited by time. In contrast to our current practice, plays could be written for presentation over several days (as were some of the medieval cycles); over an entire day, as Lindsay's play was presented, or within the scope of an evening entertainment.

Given this basic difference between narrative and drama, however, we can see that the other elements of allegory remain relatively comparable in both forms. Both are outside verisimilar time and space. Both mix abstract, typical, and historical characters in varying degrees which, again, are not subject to the demands of verisimilitude. In both, the action is episodic, achieving unity not in terms of events in the fiction nor the characters in that fiction, but through the evolving presentation of an argument which the fiction is designed to illustrate, develop, and "prove."

Such an art demands analysis which is different from the canons of modern criticism. It is clearly recognized that new attitudes toward literature developed in the later sixteenth century and produced new practices in the arts of literature which have continued in an essentially unbroken tradition since then. The obverse of that recognition is less clearly acknowledged, however: if new attitudes developed, old attitudes must have existed which will serve to explain the art of previous generations more clearly and which should make comprehensible what so often seems less than comprehensible now. Attributing what is strange to some sort of cultural primitivism which views art as essentially evolutionary is no longer a satisfactory explanation. We have learned to disregard the Renaissance vision when we look at medieval painting or sculpture; so, too, we must discard our Renaissance imagination when we come to earlier literature. It is not a question of "better" or "worse"; it is simply a matter of enlarging taste. One does not expect Giotto to be Michaelangelo; the world is large enough for both. So, too, one should not expect allegory to be the novel nor the morality play to be Shakespearean drama. Beauties may be more or less, like or unlike, but the palace of art has room for many kinds.

NOTES

1. John Skelton, *Magnyfycence*, ed. Robert Lee Ramsay, Early English Text Society, ex ser. 98 (London: Kegan Paul, Trench, Trubner and Co., 1906). John Bale, *King Johan*, ed. John Henry Pyle Pafford, Malone Society Reprints (Oxford: Oxford University Press, 1931). *Respublica*, ed., W. W. Gregg, Early English Text Society, o. s. 226 (London: Kegan Paul, Trench, Trubner and Co., 1903).

2. Once his speech is finished, the actor simply stops talking, and another actor in another part of the field attracts the audience's attention to his ensuing speech. In effect, one moves the audience, not the players. A roughly comparable method was used effectively in the recent British production of Weiss's *Marat/Sade*.

See Richard Southern's *Medieval Theatre in the Round* for a detailed reconstruction of an outdoor performance and Glynne Wickham's *Early English Stages*, vol. 1. Southern's *The Staging of Plays before Shakespeare* (London: Faber and Faber, 1973) focuses on indoor performance. Henri Rey-Flaud uses comparable hypotheses for medieval French theater in *Le Cercle Magique* (Paris: Gallimard, 1973).

3. *Respublica*, Prologue, ll. 17–18.

4. A.R. Heiserman, *Skelton and Satire*. W. O. Harris, *Skelton's Magnyfycence and the Cardinal Virtue Tradition* (Chapel Hill: University of North Carolina Press, 1965). However, David Bevington collapses the differences between Ramsay and Harris (see *Tudor Drama and Politics* [Cambridge, Mass.: Harvard University Press, 1968], pp. 54–63). Leigh Winser suggests an earlier date, possibly even ca. 1504 in "Skelton's *Magnyfycence*," *Renaissance Quarterly* 23 (1970): 14–25.

5. For our purposes, we take the text as expanded and corrected by Bale and completed about 1560. See Pafford's introduction to the Malone Society text, and W. T. Davies, "A Bibliography of John Bale," *Proceedings and Papers of the Oxford Bibliography Society* 5 (1936–37): 201–79. We must ignore the interesting questions of method posed by Bale's revisions which seem quite intelligent (see especially, the expansion of John's death scene) and decline the problems of doubling implied in the A-portion of the text. We cannot be sure of the play's form in its first production. See also Barry B. Adams's edition (San Marino, Calif.: The Huntington Library, 1969) and Thora B. Blatt, *The Plays of John Bale* (Copenhagen: G.E.C. Gad, 1968), where she dates the first version of *King Johan* "before or in 1536" (p. 21).

6. Bale describes the play as composed of two acts (ll. 1110, fol. 14 ^{a}), of two plays ("Thus endeth the ij playes of kynge Iohan," fol. 35^2), and of two

books (see Pafford's introduction to his edition, pp. xx–xxi). These terms all refer to two parts of one whole, a unity which the play certainly supports.

7. I consider an episode to begin (or end) where a major change in the nature of the action occurs.

8. Private Wealth asks Sedition "why dost þu not thy massage / & show owt of Englond, the causse of thi farre passage" (ll. 869–70).

9. This final sequence consists of six rhyme royal stanzas. The interpreter's speech, at the end of part 1, is written in five rhyme royal stanzas.

10. By historical statement, I mean the presence of Langton, Pandulphus, and Simon of Swynset. The characters of Nobility, Civil Order, and Clergy continue unchanged throughout, as do John, England, and, in his brief appearance, Commonalty.

11. Himself dying after he poisons King Johan, Dissimulation says:

> I do not doubte it, but I shall be a saynt
> Prouyde a gyldar, myne Image for to paynt
> I dye for the churche, with Thomas of Canterberye
> ye shall fast my vigyll, and vpon my daye be merye
> No doubt but I shall, do myracles in a whyle
> And therfor lete me, by shryned in the north yle.
>
> (Fol. 28 ª, ll. 2082–87)

12. This view of history seems comparable to that in the medieval cycle plays with their themes cutting across episodes representing widely separated periods of time.

13. Such judgments are, of course, merely tentative. We lack exhaustive studies of too many plays to be able to say with assurance what is "conventional" dramatic practice, what is not.

14. This may be a construction reflecting oratorical methods of narration, proof, and peroration, with the prologue functioning as the exordium. (See chapter 6.) I have not used these terms here, however, for I think a detailed study of the terms as they were used in contemporary discussions of drama is necessary before one can be sure of their exact reference. To use them at this preliminary stage of discussion would only cloud the analysis.

15. While this describes the basic outline of the action, one can see that the first two parts are further divided. The first episode includes two related parts, that concerning Sensualitie and that including the vices. The second episode is divided into a short sequence around Veritie and a longer set of scenes organized around the fortunes of Chastitie.

16. Chapter 3, pp. 79–80.

17. See chapter 1, pp. 16–22.

18. Edwin S. Miller discusses this scene in detail in "The Christening of the *Three Estates*," *MLN* 60 (1945): 42–44.

19. Cf. the description of Wishart's trial, discussed in chapter 2, pp. 47–50.

Chapter 6

The Morality Reconsidered

Often, this sort of book begins with a brief "review of the literature," a scholarly practice which can become a mere, tedious list, as tedious to compile as it is to read. Yet such review is essential to research, for through it we locate the ideas and assumptions which characterize the current approach. Work on the morality play (with some notable exceptions) is still dominated by ideas developed at the turn of the century. These ideas continue as assumptions in much current research, despite signs that some are beginning to find them less than satisfactory.[1] Thus, if we are to escape from the specific for a moment and enlarge the implications of this study to the treatment of the morality play in general, it becomes necessary to examine the assumptions of others as well as my own.

By their very nature, assumptions are the most difficult elements to track down. Usually, they are those truths which are taken to be self-evident, so evident they are not worth the time to argue or even, in many cases, to state. This book is shaped by three basic assumptions. It assumes that the morality play is primarily dramatic allegory and primarily didactic. It also assumes that the vernacular materials of the late Middle Ages provide implicit evidence and a literary tradition which will explain the dramatic practices of the morality play as it existed in the fifteenth and sixteenth centuries. In such a context, then, this book turns from the question of Renaissance influence and searches instead among the materials in the native tradition, so many of which remain unexplored while classical and continental sources are scoured for new intimations.

With these assumptions, I have examined the nature of allegorical plot, that tissue of action and character designed to convey not so much emotional response as intellectual response—the response that comes from understanding a topic or a human situation in a new way which is proposed by the author. This is a matter not so much of one soul working on others through the emotions as of one mind working on others through its organization and presentation of ideas. Within this approach, I have argued that allegorical plot—both narrative and dramatic—is essentially an expository art, embodying argument in action. This relationship produces a resultant lack of emphasis on extended characterization. In the process, we have seen both the widely different kinds of materials which are embodied in late medieval allegory and the widely different treatments of essentially similar materials. Underlying all of this is an assumption that didactic literature *is* interesting, and an acceptance of the Horatian attitude (so long taken as truth in English literature) that art may teach *and* please. Or, turning the phrase a bit, that the exercise of the intellect may be as entertaining and delightful as the play on emotional response.

Such statements border on cliché, perhaps, yet they seem necessary at a time when literary criticism, in general, has been dominated by the overvaluation of fine language and dense texture, or, more lately, by a search for common patterns based on modern psychology—whether Oedipal or archetypal.[2] Despite the fact that men continue to teach and preach through literature, the last hundred years have seen a profusion of literary theories which stem from the "art-for-art's sake" attitude and which viewed the didactic as a threat to "pure" literary value. Coupled with this attitude was the essentially evolutionary view of literature, a view which sees literary genres as subject to a process of birth, growth to maturity, and subsequent decay. With such attitudes, late medieval literature became the natural source for studies in the evolutionary view, and, since the literature is so heavily didactic, it also became the natural place to search for the shift to nondidactic literary values, a shift often connected with the "growth of secularism."

Because the morality play has rarely been studied for the sake of that drama alone, current scholarship is still under the sway of authorities who sought the origins of the characterization and mimetic plot valued in Elizabethan drama.[3] The central idea to emerge from these studies, produced for the most part in the first quarter or so of this century, is the "psychomachia principle," an idea which informs both the most influential book so far produced on medieval allegory,

Lewis's *The Allegory of Love* and most recent studies of the morality play. Returning to the earliest statements of the psychomachia principle, we may find that idea most conveniently stated in the often-cited monograph, "The English Moral Play," published by E. N. S. Thompson in 1910.[4]

The center of Thompson's interest lies in the origins of the morality play. He attributes the drama's ultimate impulse to Prudentius's *Psychomachia*, although he is careful to note that only vestigial traces of the epic battle of vices and virtues appear in the morality play. (Indeed, only one short battle literally occurs at all, and that is in the *Castle of Perseverance*.) Nevertheless, Prudentius is the "father of the morality play" because "he established . . . the idea upon which all those plays were based." [5] Despite the substitution of the "realism of everyday life for the romance of the outworn epic," the plays were "in spirit and in general plan . . . only a retelling of the fourth-century allegorical epic" (p. 333). Thompson's basis for this judgment lies primarily in an analysis of the *Castle of Perseverance* as a psychomachia, a kind of archetype or basic model for the single topic of the morality play: the battle of virtues and vices for the soul of man. Thus we have the "full-scope morality plan," a definition based on four extant plays *(The Castle of Perseverance, Mankind, Wisdom, Everyman)*, a fragment *(Pride of Life)*, and passing references to the lost Pater Noster plays.[6]

It should be evident from this admittedly bald compression that Thompson's argument depends on certain assumptions which may be overlooked when a view becomes authoritative. Most obvious is the fact that Thompson bases his definition on those extant plays which are dated before 1500.[7] After that date, he treats the early Tudor drama as a series of departures from his basic model. Such a division derives from the medieval-Renaissance division in English history, a view which is less authoritative today.[8] Beyond that, however, the heavy emphasis on the *Castle of Perseverance* seems to result from its position as the first complete surviving text, even though the *Pride of Life*, with its royal cast, suggests that other kinds of "protagonists" existed besides the "unindividualized" Man, as the hero of that morality which "was destined to disappear in the freer spirit and broader knowledge of the Renaissance" (p. 359).

But more tenuous assumptions cling to Thompson's essay and continue to clog recent discussions of the morality play, despite indications that we are moving toward a more flexible view of the drama. Approaching the *Castle of Perseverance*, Thompson cautions the reader, one "should remember that its author and its first audiences knew nothing of the drama *qua* drama, and should study it first, according to its intention, as a piece of didactic literature, a 'sermo corporeus' " (p. 320). Later, discussing the "entirely undidactic spirit" of Heywood's dramas, Thompson sees that

> once this type of play was introduced, the days of the morality were numbered, not primarily because of its superior godliness, but rather because of its abstention from the theme most interesting to humanity—human life. The rule of allegory in literature had been long, and its reach wide; it was now compelled to yield to the reawakened sense of the dignity and the wealth of secular thought and secular life. (p. 389)

However much we may admire the learning that accompanies such statements, they are typical of a preconceived idea of the nature of drama which ultimately stems from theories underlying the modern "well-made play." Thus, drama is the representation of conflict between characters, arranged in a pattern of action rising, through complication, to a climax and subsequent denouement. Besides assuming a fixed dramatic pattern, such statements, by implication, legislate subject matter and method of setting up a series of opposites: secularism vs. religion, reality vs. allegory, drama vs. didacticism.

Of course, these terms are not really mutually exclusive. Yet, when one finds them employed in the history of the drama, the result is often a confusing account of varying classifications and of shifting evaluations. Still, such observations can be turned to new uses. If the early drama is allegorical, if it is didactic, then these are the characteristics of artistic method and effect which should be explored, and which I have attempted to explore in this book. I have suggested that the crux of the allegorical method lies *not* in the relationship between character and action, but in the relationship between action and theme. This is a matter of differing emphases. In mimetic literature, the primary interest lies in the fable, the bare sketch of simple events which might appear in a *précis* or in a writer's first notes before he actually creates the narrative. That simple action is expanded to provide precise character and detailed motivation. In other words, the whole effort is toward verisimilitude, and the theme, in its larger relevance, grows out of the action by implication. In didactic efforts, however, fable is subsidiary to theme, the topic or abstract argument which develops as the narrative progresses and which controls the order and shape of the episodes that constitute the action. Here, we are not interested in the story per se (although, of course, we expect to find it capable of holding our attention): what primarily holds our attention is what the action *means*. That is, the true action of the didactic work is not the surface events, but the action of the unfolding argument. This, in turn, suggests that didactic art is essentially expository; that is, its effects are designed for exposition of, and persuasion to, a thesis, a particular point of view.

But such an alteration in the relation between fable and theme also suggests an alteration in the relation between action and character. Most discussions of allegorical character make a distinction between abstract and typical characters, between characters like Veritie and Rex Humanitas in the *Thrie Estaitis*.[9] In some allegories, the characters include historical figures, like Bale's *King Johan* or Dante's *Comedia*. This group includes the biblical moralities, for *Queen Hester* and Wagner's *Mary Magdalene* use "historical" persons as well as abstract and typical figures. Yet, given a plot which is controlled by theme and not by the depiction of character, such distinctions seem elementary. Allegorical character is not verisimilar in the sense that the authors do not show us the slow development and shift of personality over an extended facsimile of time and space. We are given a group of what E. M. Forster might have called "flat" characters who function as a set of "signs"; i.e., these characters represent kinds of behavior and kinds of experiences which the writer uses as terms in his developing argument and which the audience recognizes as such. In effect, the playwright depends on his audience to recognize the intellectual implications of a character named "Divine Correctioun"; for the purposes of his argument, he has no need to give us a full depiction of personality because we already know what the character represents.

Given this view of a different relationship between character, action, and theme, we may now return to the view of drama as a representation of conflict between characters, arranged in a pattern of action rising, through complication, to a climax and denouement. The limits of that approach are evident both in the view of the morality play as psychomachia and in the later perception of a "rise-fall-rise" pattern of action, a description which describes the fortune of the protagonist. Certainly, the rise-fall-rise pattern appears in enough of the plays to be a familiar outline.[10] Certainly, the plays show conflict between virtues and vices. Certainly, both descriptions are rather primitive. We could describe any drama as a conflict between good and evil, which is what the virtues and vices represent, after all. And tragedy could be described as a simple rise-and-fall pattern. Both statements are true enough, but they tell us nothing about the individual kinds of artistic differences which make Greek drama different from Elizabethan drama, *King Lear* different from *Macbeth*, or Shaw's *Saint Joan* from the Digby *Mary Magdalene*. Nor does the protagonist-antagonist scheme of analysis take us very far. Characterization is relatively minimal in the morality play, and even if we manage to erect a protagonist in a Mankind or a King, his antagonists generally appear as part of a group which is just as much opposed to another group as they are to the "hero." Distinguishing between morality plays on the basis of story, of fable, then, has been and is a frustrating task, in good part because the fables are relatively simple and relatively similar.

We are left, then, with the area of theme. But if our usual canons of dramatic criticism, based on conflict, are feeble, how are we to discuss the morality play? Even our terms, *theme, character, action* are tools of mimetic drama and are used here analogically in order to describe a different kind of literary construct.

Perhaps we might begin by remembering that drama, in its barest definition, simply means "that which is presented on stage." We might next ask, for each play, "What is presented on stage?" and then frame our answers, not in terms of action or of a simple "moral," but in terms of the much more complex didactic theme. Lawrence V. Ryan, in his exemplary analysis of *Everyman*, does just that when he rejects the simple-minded formulation of "do good deeds and you will be saved" in favor of a precise thematic summation. The play, he states, is "a concise representation of the orthodox teaching on the matter of man's salvations." [11] Such a summation is not as simple as it seems in extract, for the terms take on new meanings as a result of the research which reconstructs the contemporary idea and demonstrates how the particular view set forth in the play parallels or departs from comparable views. So William O. Harris's analysis of *Magnificence* as a play about fortitude only takes on meaning within the context of the medieval view of the virtues.[12]

Once that problem of sheer meaning is solved, we are still left with the questions of dramatic form and the problem of learning how to look at a drama foreign to most modern critical theories. The tendency, of course, is to begin to invent categories, but this is not, I believe, the best solution. Such invention serves, as it does here, the purpose of preliminary investigation when one is simply trying to see what the episodes are and how they fit together, but such an effort seems unlikely to lead into the subsequent evaluation of quality. We want to know not only what the writers did but what they thought they were doing, for the latter often throws light on the former. In other words, we need to know something about contemporary aesthetic theories and how those theories relate to the drama of the time. Yet, although a body of commentary on the drama exists for later periods, no such aids to comprehension have turned up for the pre-Shakespearean English drama.

Nevertheless, we may still reconstruct a valid dramatic aesthetic, based on contemporary sources. The materials, I believe, lie within the current exploration of medieval rhetoric, coupled with commentaries on the Latin drama. Studies such as Marvin T. Herrick's *Comic Theory in the Sixteenth Century* imply a profitable road for further exploration. While his inevitable center of interest is the development of Elizabethan dramatic theory,[13] Herrick does tell us that two schemes for plot analysis existed before the rediscovery of Aristotle's *Poetics*. One, inherited from Donatus, divided the play into the familiar *prologue, protasis, epitasis, catastrophe*. Another existed, however, and was used by fifteenth- and early sixteenth-century commentators on Terence. This method derives from the analysis of oratory and sees the play in terms of *exordium, narration, proof, conclusion*. The terms are fairly clear and are essentially the pattern we still practice: an introduction, a narration or statement of the problem, a consideration of the evidence or "proofs" for one's view of the problem, and the subsequent conclusion. What is strange about this, of course, is its application to drama, yet a comment like Philip Melanchthon's on the *Andria* appears to assume such an approach: "The whole play is like the persuasive type of oration; for old men, young men, and servants deliberate on the whole matter in various ways." [14] While Herrick's book provides such tantalizing tidbits, they function only as a point of departure for his main description. He tells us that fifteenth-century commentaries on the plays of Terence exist, but few have mined them for their relevance to criticism of the drama, both that produced in neo-Latin and in the vernacular.[15] In part, this neglect may be the result of Creizenach's influence, for even as careful and erudite a scholar as Mary Marshall tells us that "the main mediaeval error was in interpreting the method of representing Roman plays as a form of recitation, sometimes with accompanying miming. . . . Creizenach and other historians of the drama have emphasized the seriousness of this mistake, because it meant that the plays of Terence which were known did not in general . . . serve as effective dramatic models." [16] Such an observation suggests that a turnabout may be necessary. Perhaps the error lies in our modern view of how Terence should serve as an effective dramatic model.

The comprehension of such commentaries depends, further, on the comprehension of pre-Elizabethan rhetoric, in general. This means the categories which explain the exposition and development of a thesis (*not* the uses of language or figure which usually occupy half a rhetorical treatise). Like the morality play, medieval rhetoric is still relatively unexplored. As long ago as 1942, Richard McKeon pointed out the limitations of existing work; his "Rhetoric in the Middle Ages" opens with a devastatingly ironic summary of the most authoritative books on the subject.[17] Since then, some promising work has been done, but its specific relevance to the morality play is limited. The reason for this is simple: the period during which the morality flourished falls between two stools in literary study. Dated, roughly, between 1400 and 1560 or so, the morality play is part of that neglected period which is only beginning to be studied as the sharp division of medieval-Renaissance loses its hold over historians—literary and otherwise. Since this is the case, books on sixteenth-century rhetoric begin from an ill-defined base around 1500 and rapidly proceed to their real business: the description of ideas on rhetoric which found their general milieu during Shakespeare's time. This emphasis generally (and quite understandably) results in the neglect of older ideas. The other area, centered around Chaucer, may be taken as too early for our purposes, yet it is here that glimpses of promising ideas exist, if their history during the "interim" period between Chaucer and Shakespeare can be worked out.

We can see this in a discussion of allegory by Robert L. Montgomery when he quotes Boccaccio's remark that "fiction is a form of discourse which, under guise of invention, illustrates or proves an idea; and, as its superficial aspect is removed, the meaning of the author is clear." [18] While Boccaccio's comment comes in the context of his discussion of the interpretation of classical myth (the *Geneology*), it supports Montgomery's contention that *allegory* has three distinct references in medieval usage: (1) to refer to the fourfold method of interpretation; (2) to describe an element of style, the use of *inversio* and extended metaphor; and (3) to describe "the nature of the whole fiction or fable," a nature which is usually associated with "the incredible or patently untrue" (p. 45). It is the third category, the nature of the whole fiction or fable, which parallels the approach to allegory taken in this book, and Boccaccio's connection between discourse and fiction appears to verify the relationship between theme and action in allegorical plot. Interestingly enough, a comparable distinction turns up in Douglas Kelly's observation that "for Geoffrey [of Vinsauf] *thema* is the theme or subject the author is going to develop, *materia* the content of the poem established after consideration of the *thema*."[19] Despite the differences in terminology, it is evident that both Boccaccio and Geoffrey are making a distinction between the intellectual content of a fiction and the story or invented action. If such a distinction holds true for the morality play as well as for narrative allegory, it seems evident that most criticism of this drama has proceeded on the basis of Montgomery's second category: allegory as extended metaphor. Such an emphasis inevitably leads us to emphasize the invention of the fable. What I propose, then, is a shift of emphasis from the examination of allegory as "extended metaphor" to a consideration of allegory as a "form of discourse" where the theme controls the nature of the *materia*. Such a shift may move us beyond the quagmire of similar fables to the perception of other differences.

For example, Lewis divides allegory into two categories: the "allegory of love" and a residual category which he calls "moral" or "homiletic." Surely, courtly love with all its attendant chivalry has been the area of medieval literature most studied and most appreciated, and Lewis's book, in large part, joined the allegory to the popularity of the romance.[20] Yet Lewis's categories seem unbalanced. That allegory treated questions of love is a fact no one would deny, but that all other allegories may be labeled "moral allegory" or "mixed allegory" seems less useful, particularly when one sees the variety of topics and treatments accorded to even the ten texts discussed here (chapters 3 and 4). Like the term *moral play*, moral allegory does not take us very far. Since this is the case, perhaps we need more extensive study of those "other" allegories before we can safely assign them to categories.

What we are saying, then, is that allegory is a *mode*, a way of making fictions which are used for other purposes than the purely mimetic. As a mode, it cannot really be defined in terms of the specific topics it treats nor even in terms of the specific effects it produces, since these are subject to variation. Of course one can call allegory "extended metaphor," although the term is too often taken as an invitation to describe "what stands for what" with its resultant emphasis on personification, and thus on character. In Lewis's more sophisticated view, the extended metaphor becomes an equivalence between the action of the allegory and a state of mind, so that what we have is, in effect, an externalized representation of an internal struggle, another definition of the psychomachia which assumes the mimetic nature of allegory. Rosemund Tuve quite rightly objects to such a psychological description,[21] and, like Lewis's book, hers is full of sensitive and sympathetic responses to allegories which have found few champions. Yet her continued use of the view that allegory is "extended metaphor" continues to emphasize the fable at the expense of the theme. This does not mean that such readers miss the point of an individual allegory. Many scholars have noted, almost incidentally, the importance of the argument as an integral part of the allegory,[22] but no one has worked out the consequences which this importance has for the art of allegory.

Perhaps the definition of allegory as extended metaphor has a sufficiently poetic ring which enables us to avoid meeting the questions of didactic art. Indeed, until fairly recently, that term *didactic art* would be regarded as a paradox in some literary quarters where art could not mean, but must simply be. The recent development of interest in the morality play suggests that we may be ready to look at the uses of didactic art without apologies. Yet, if we are to do so, new methods and new materials must be developed. The plays have too long been treated in isolation from their contemporary literary background, and as long as we neglect how men thought about literature in the fifteenth and early sixteenth centuries, we can make few judgments about literary value. Without that objective basis, we are left with essentially subjective standards of judgment. Thus, we seem to judge quality in the pre-Shakespearean drama essentially on the basis of which plays bore us and which do not, or, more objectively, which plays provide analogues for the later drama and thus gain a specious sort of value having little to do with the aesthetics of the time in which they were written. Given such aesthetics, literary historians may still prefer Elizabethan drama—it is hard to imagine anything else—yet, in the process, we may widen our taste and deepen our understanding.

It is evident, then, that the current confused definitions of the morality play stands only for lack of a better one, and that the division of the catalogue of plays into a small pre-1500 group and a large post-1500 group (reflecting the medieval-Renaissance division of British history) generates a simplified view of that drama which reduces it to psychomachia. It is more than that, and that *more* takes us into the very areas many scholars have found distasteful in the past: the nondramatic literature of the fifteenth and early sixteenth centuries which provides many of the analogues and much of the context of the drama, the nature of allegory and of didactic drama, both in the realm of practical criticism and of aesthetic theory.

If it is indeed time to reconsider the morality play, that reconsideration will undoubtedly require the work of many scholars. It will take time before even that most important of tasks is completed: the production of texts, edited and annotated in terms of modern scholarship. Anyone who struggles with this drama must also struggle with large areas of ignorance—both his own and that of the hardly examined era he studies. The problem is a familiar one, common to all literary study. The text one chooses seems inexhaustible, for it leads its attentive reader into other genres besides the one he is attempting to understand; into other histories besides the literary history he might hope to master; into other analytic skills which demand tools different from those he has mastered. Help in the more tangible form of detailed studies seems all too frequently nonexistent. The pilgrim in the land of the morality play must indeed hope that Grace appears to help his feeble efforts. This book is, quite simply, an attempt to understand one play, as a means toward understanding others like it. It is, I hope, a little informed by that abstract, personified virtue called grace and not too hampered by those other vices which figure in our modern intellectual psychomachia.

NOTES

1. In this chapter, I shall discuss and note only examples of the basic views connected with the morality play. For bibliography, see Carl Stratman's *Bibliography of Medieval Drama*, 2d ed. (New York: Frederick Ungar, 1972), and P. J. Houle's bibliography, *The English Morality and Related Drama* (Hamden, Conn.: The Shoe String Press, 1972).

2. Despite their differences, C. S. Lewis and Rosemund Tuve practice a form of criticism which emphasizes stylistics (e.g. "imagery," "metaphor,"

"fine style") as the central element of literature. For an example of the anthropological approach, see Angus Fletcher's *Allegory, the Theory of a Symbolic Mode* (Ithaca: Cornell University Press, 1964). Although such theories probably affect medieval studies less heavily than more modern periods, they do influence the current student's view of earlier literature. For Renaissance hermetic allegory, see Don Cameron Allen's *Mysteriously Meant* (Baltimore: Johns Hopkins Press, 1970), and Michael Murrin, *The Veil of Allegory* (Chicago: University of Chicago Press, 1969). Murrin's approach has much in common with Fletcher's. James I. Wimsatt takes a structural approach in *Allegory and Mirror: Tradition and Structure in Middle English Literature* (New York: Pegasus Press, 1971).

3. See, however, "*Controversia* in the English Drama: Medwall and Massinger," *PMLA* 68 (1953): 286–303, where Eugene M. Waith argues for a reconsideration of form in Elizabethan drama, based on an examination of traditional rhetoric. Wolfgang Clemen's treatment of *Gorboduc* also makes interesting use of rhetorical analysis. See his *English Tragedy before Shakespeare*, trans. T. S. Dorsch (London: Methuen & Co., 1961). Both scholars work largely from the classical rhetoricians.

4. E.N.S. Thompson, "The English Moral Play," *Transactions of the Connecticut Academy of Arts and Sciences* 14 (1908–10): 291–415. Bernard Spivack in his *Shakespeare and the Allegory of Evil* (New York: Columbia University Press, 1958) coined the phrase *psychomachia principle*, a term subsequently adopted by David Bevington in *From Mankind to Marlowe* (Cambridge, Mass.: Harvard University Press, 1962). These two books, along with Bevington's *Tudor Drama and Politics* and F. P. Wilson's *The English Drama 1485–1585* (Oxford: The Clarendon Press, 1969) are the most recent surveys of the morality play. All rely basically on the view of alleogry characteristic of Thompson and Lewis. Fore more detailed study of allegory, one must turn to the work on specific texts; e.g., *Piers Plowman, The Faerie Queene*. Edgar T. Schell's work reflects a serious effort to rethink the categories. (He seems to be influenced by Northrup Frye.) See his "On the Imitation of Life's Pilgrimage in *The Castle of Perseverance*," (*Journal of English and Germanic Philology* 67 [1968]: 235–48) and his introduction (with J. D. Schuchter) to the student text, *English Morality Plays and Moral Interludes* (New York: Holt, Rhinehart and Winston, 1969).

5. According to A. P. Rossiter, Creizenach was the first to trace the morality play to Prudentius (*English Drama from the Earliest Times to Elizabeth*, p. 95). See also Lewis's discussion of Prudentius in chapter 2 of the *Allegory of Love*.

6. Writing in 1378 in his *De Officio Pastorali*, John Wycliffe refers to the teaching of the Pater Noster "in English tunge as men seyen in the pleye of Yorke." This may be the earliest reference to a morality play. See Wickham, *Early English Stages*, 1:144, 230 ff., but cf. Hardin Craig, *English Religious Drama* (Oxford: The Clarendon Press, 1955), p. 338 ff. It is perhaps gratuitous to note that, of the four plays, three are the Macro moralities, discovered

together. Certainly, we have no control over survival, but the demon of accidental and fragmented evidence remains a problem.

7. Henry Medwall's *Nature* (1495?) is "touched by the spirit of humanism" (p. 332). *Fulgens and Lucrece* (1497?) had not been discovered when Thompson wrote his essay. Donald C. Baker, in "The Date of Mankind" (*Philological Quarterly* 42 [1963]: 90–91) establishes 1464–69 as the range for one of the earliest moralities. *Wisdom* is dated 1450–1500? *Everyman*, 1495? Thus, the *Castle of Perseverance* and the *Pride of Life* (1400–25?) are the earliest. I use T. W. Craik's chronology here, as a convenient reference; see his *The Tudor Interlude*, pp. 140–41. See also Alfred Harbage's *Annals of English Drama, 975–1700*, rev. ed. by S. Schoenbaum (London: Methuen & Co., 1964), which contains a chronological list and guide to editions.

8. See historian Lacey Baldwin Smith's "The 'Taste for Tudors' Since 1940," in *Changing Views on British History: Essays on Historical Writing Since 1939*, ed. Elizabeth C. Furber (Cambridge, Mass.: Harvard University Press, 1966). Smith observes that "most early Tudor scholarship [in history] is grounded upon the quagmire of the fifteenth century, which of all eras is the least understood or studied" (p. 115). A comparable state of affairs exists in English studies. In providing the chronological table for *Chaucer and the Fifteenth Century* (Oxford: Oxford University Press, 1954), H. S. Bennett notes that "the dates of many . . . works are disputed, and a question-mark necessarily appears after many titles. The dates even to works to which no question-mark is attached are often conjectural and should be understood as merely approximate" (p. 219).

Many of the morality plays are in a similar state, and, often enough, the date of printing is used without clarification. Such uncertainties about objective facts complicate the difficulties of evaluating relationships between plays, and, often, the plays themselves. Moreover, the classifications of drama may themselves need rethinking; for example, the sharp divisions between "miracle," "morality," and "mystery" plays. William F. Host has edited *Lucidus and Dubius* and *Occupation, Idleness and Doctrine* which have been classified as "dialogues" (see his Ph.D. diss., Ohio State University, 1974). He argues that both were performed, apparently for schoolboys. They appear in Winchester College MS no. 33, which Host dates 1430–60. The second (above) has numerous parallels to sixteenth-century plays, like *Youth and Hickscorner*. Norman Davis has recently re-edited *Non-Cycle Plays and Fragments* (Early English Text Society [London: Oxford University Press, 1970]), which prints four newly included fragments.

9. W. R. Mackenzie's *The English Moralities from the Point of View of Allegory*, Harvard Studies in English, 2 (Boston: Ginn and Co., 1914) is the standard expression of this distinction for the morality play, although it is outdated. For more recent discussions of this distinction, see Robert W. Frank, Jr.'s, "The Art of Reading Medieval Personification Allegory," pp. 237–50, Arnold

William's "The English Moral Play before 1500," in *Annuale Mediaevale*, Duquesne Studies, 4 (Pittsburgh, 1963), pp. 5–22, and W. T. H. Jackson's "Allegory and Allegorization," *Research Studies* (Washington State University) 32 (1964): 161–75.

10. This view originated with Willard Farnham's *The Medieval Heritage of Elizabethan Tragedy* and is incorporated in his examination of earlier drama by Irving Ribner in *The English History Play in the Age of Shakespeare* (Princeton: Princeton University Press, 1957; rev. ed. New York: Barnes and Noble, 1965). One must remember, of course, that Farnham was describing what he saw as a philosophic change in the view of experience and is thus analyzing the drama in terms of its content of ideas, not in terms of form.

11. Lawrence V. Ryan, "Doctrine and Dramatic Structure in *Everyman*," *Speculum* 32 (1957): 722–35.

12. Harris, *Skelton's Magynfycence and the Cardinal Virtue Tradition.*

13. See, for example, chapter 4, "The Conception of Plot in the Sixteenth Century" and p. 89, where Herrick limits his major inquiry to the "well-made plot" (*Comic Theory in the Sixteenth Century* [Urbana: University of Illinois Press, 1950]).

14. As quoted by Herrick, ibid., p. 73.

15. Certainly, the long-neglected contemporary Latin drama must be studied as well as the commentaries. Leicester Bradner provides a fine introduction in two articles: "The Latin Drama of the Renaissance (1340–1640,)" *Studies in the Renaissance* 4 (1957): 31–70, which includes a bibliography of neo-Latin drama to 1650, and, in a joint report with Louis A. Schuster, "Neo-Latin Drama: Two Views of Opportunities. (1) Pioneering in Neo-Latin Drama, (2) Desiderata for the Study of Neo-Latin Drama," in *Renaissance Drama, A Report on Research Opportunities,* ed. S. Schoenbaum, 6 (1963): 14–20. See also Lily B. Campbell, *Divine Poetry and Drama in Sixteenth-Century England* (Berkeley: University of California Press, 1959, pp. 141–260.

16. Mary Marshall, "Theatre in the Middle Ages: Evidence from Dictionaries and Glosses," *Symposium* (Syracuse University) 4 (1950): 375.

17. Richard McKeon, "Rhetoric in the Middle Ages," *Speculum* 17 (1942): 1–32. For more current bibliography, see J. J. Murphy, *Medieval Rhetoric,* Toronto Medieval Bibliographies, 3 (University of Toronto Press, 1971).

18. Robert L. Montgomery, "Allegory and the Incredible Fable: The Italian View from Dante to Tasso," *PMLA* 81 (1966): 46. Translated text from *Boccaccio on Poetry*, ed. and trans, C. G. Osgood (New York: Columbia University Press, 1956), p. 48.

19. Douglas Kelly, "The Scope of the Treatment of Composition in the Twelfth and Thirteenth Century Arts of Poetry," *Speculum* 41 (1966): 272. See also James J. Murphy, "Literary Implications of Instruction in the Verbal Arts in Fourteenth Century England," *Leeds Studies in English* 1 (1967): 119–35, and his *Rhetoric in the Middle Ages* (Berkeley: University of California Press, 1974).

20. Both these elements figure in the *Faerie Queene* where Spenser provides a culmination for historians of allegory just as Shakespeare provides the culmination for historians of the drama. Like Lewis's book, Rosemund Tuve's *Allegorical Imagery* (Princeton: Princeton University Press, 1966) embodies an effort to understand medieval allegory in order to explain Spenser.

21. See ibid., p. 252 ff.

22. E. G., Bevington, *From Mankind to Marlowe*, pp. 3–4; Fletcher, *Allegory*, pp. 220–21; Harris, *Skelton's Magnyfycence*, p. 10; Spivack, *Shakespeare and the Allegory of Evil*, pp. 176–77; Tuve, *Allegorical Imagery*, p. 199; Wickham, *Early English Stages*, 1:230. See also Bloomfield, "Allegory as Interpretation," pp. 309–10, and Peter Saccio, *The Court Comedies of John Lyly: A Study in Allegorical Dramaturgy* (Princeton: Princeton University Press, 1969).

Werner Habicht's emphasis on theme is probably the most pronounced in recent work. See his *Studien zur Dramenform vor Shakespeare* (Heidelberg: Anglistische Forschungen, 1969), and his excellent thematic analysis, "The Wit Interlude," *Renaissance Drama* 8 (1965): 73–88. My article, "Dramatic Allegory, or, Exploring the Moral Play" (*Comparative Drama* 7 [1973]: 68–82), briefly summarizes the argument presented in this book.

Appendix

Sir William Eure's Letter[1]

[Fol. 137*a*] Pleas it your goode Lordeshipe to be advertisede that at the meating whiche I had with twoe gentle men of the King of scotts Counsaile at Caldestreme for suche buysynes as I haue aduertised your lordshipe of in myn other lettre with of our procedings in the same / I hade diuerse commynyngs with Mr Thomas Bellendyn one of the saide [C]oun[ce]llours for scotlande / a man by estymacion apperaunte to be of thage of fiftye yeres or above / and of gentle and sage conversacion / specially touching the staye / of the spritualtie in scotlande / and gathering hym to be a [man] inclyned to the soorte vsed in our souerains Realme of England / I dide soe largely breke with hym in thoes behalues / as to move to knowe of hym of whate mynde the King and counsaile of scotland was inclyned unto / concernyng the busshope of Rome / and for the reformacion of the mysusing of the spritualtie in scotlande / wherunto he genttlie and lovinglie aunswered / shewing hym self well contented of that commynyng / did saye that the King of scotts hym self / with all his temporall Counsaile was gretely geven to the reformacion of the mysdemeanours of Busshops / Religious persones / and preists within the Realme / And so muche that by the Kings pleasour / he being prevey therunto / thay haue hade ane enterluyde played in the feaste of the epiphanne of our lorde laste paste / before the King and Quene at Lighgive / and the hoole counsaile sprituall and temporall / The hoole matier whereof concluded vpon the Declaracion of the noughtines in Religion / the presumpcion of busshops /The collucion of the sprituall Courts / called the concistory courts in scotland / and mysusing of preists / I haue obteigned a noote frome a scotts man of our

~ 147 ~

sorte / being present at the playing of the saide enterluyde / of theffecte therof / whiche I doe sende vnto your lordeshipe by this berer / My lorde the same Mr Bellendyn shewed me that after the said enterluyd fynished the King of scotts Dide call vpon the busshope of Glascoe being Chauncelour and diuerse other busshops / exorting thaym to reforme thair facions and maners of lyving / saying that oneles they soe did / he wold sende sex of the proudeste of thaym vnto his vncle of england / and as thoes wer ordoured soe he wold ordour all the reste / that wolde not a mende and therunto the Chauncelour shuld aunswer / and say vnto the King that one worde of his graces mouthe shuld suffice thayme to be at commaundement / and the king haistely and angrely aunswered that he wold gladely bestowe any words of his mouthe that could a mend thaym / I am alsoe aduertised by the same Mr bellendyn / that the King of scottes is fully mynded to expell all spirtuall men frome having any auctoritie by office vnder his grace / either in household or elles where within the Realme / And Dailye studiethe and devisithe for that entente / The same Mr bellendyne / haithe desired of me / to haue an abstracte of all suche Actes constitucions and proclamacions as ar passed within this the King [Fol. 137b] our Soverains Realme touching the suppression of Religion / and gather[ing] unto the Kinges maiestie suche other proffeites / as befor haithe been sp[ritual] with the reformacion of the mysdemeanours of the clergye / saying that h[e] trustethe to haue the King his Master to studie the same / And haith m[ ] me that if I cane attaigne the saide Actes constitucions and Proclamac[ions] that I shall not adventur to sende hym thame / but by suche a pr[evy] persone as he by a secreate token whiche is devised bitwene hy[m and] me shall send vnto me / for that purpose / Ffurther he haithe aduert[ised] me / that it is appointed the quene of scottes now being with child[e] shalbe Crowned on sondaye the firste Daye of Februarij And thereafter shalbe had a Convencion of the lordes / for whate purpoos [I] cannote be certefied as yet / but as is thought apertely for the reform[a]cion of spritualtie / I am aduertised by one of myn espielles that the Kinge of scottes having at this instaunte three shipes in redynes to goe t[o] the sees / haithe been at seen and viewed the same / and that it is Rumered a mainges the common people / thay shulde be prepairede for the King to goe to the meating in france / My lord conscidering theffectes of the premisses / I thought my duetie could be noe les thene of the same with deligence to aduertise your lordeshipe / wherin as shall further stande with the King*es* maiesties plea*sur* to com*m*aunde me / even soe I shall god willing applie myn vtter deligence / by the grace of the hollie gooste / whoe ever pres*er*ue your goode lordshipe / At the King*es* maiesties Castell of Berwike / the xxvjth Daye of Januarye / your lordships /

At com*m*aundement

Wyllm Eure

[Endorsement, Fol. 139*a*, the original cover, verso blank] To the right hon*o*rable and my very goode Lorde my Lord*es* prevey seale.

[Top right hand corner]   seale from the Captayn of Berwyke

[Enclosure, Fol. 138*a*]

The Copie of the nootes of the interluyde

I*n* the first entres come in **Solaice** / whose parte was but to make mery / sing ballett*es* with his ffelowes / and Drinke at the interluyd*es* of the play [/] whoe shewede firste to all the audience the playe to be played / whiche was a gen*er*all thing / meanyng nothing in speciall to displeas noe man / praying therfor noe man to be angre *with* the same. **Nexte** come in a King / whoe passed to his throne / having noe speche to thende of the playe / and thene to ratefie and approve as in playne p*ar*liament all thing*es* doon by the reste of the players whiche represented the Thre estes / Withe hym come his c*our*tiour*s* **Placebo** / **Pikthanke** / and **fflaterye** / and suche a like garde / one swering he was the lustieste / starkeste / best pr*o*porcioned and moste valiaunte man that ever was / An other swear*ing* he was the beste *with* longe bowe / Crosebowe / and Culverein in the world / An other swear*ing* he was the best Juster / and man of Armes in the world / and soe furthe during thair p*ar*tes / **Ther after** came a man / armed in harnes / with a sword drawen in his hande / **A Busshope** / **A Burges** man / and **Experience** / clede like a docto*ur* / whoe sete thaym all down on the deis / vnder the **King** / After thayme come a poor **Man** / whoe did goe vpe and downe the scaffald / making a

hevie complaynte / that he was heryed throughe the courtiours taking
his fewe in one place / and alsoe his tackes in an other place / wher
throughe he hade strayled his house / his wif and childeren beg-
gyng their brede / and soe of many thousaund in scotlande / whiche
wolde make the **Kynges** grace lose of men if his grace stod neide /
saying thair was noe remedye to be gotten / for thoughe he wolde
suyte to the kinges grace / he was naither acquaynted with controuller
nor treasurer / and without thaym myght noe man gete noe goodenes
of the king / And after he spered for the king / And whene he was
showed to the **man** that was **king** in the playe / he aunsuered and
said he was noe king / ffor ther is but one king / whiche made all
and gouernethe / all / whoe is eternall / to whome he and all erthely
kinges ar but officers / of the whiche thay muste make recknyng /
and so furthe muche moor to that effect / And thene he loked to
the **king** and saide he was not the king of scotlande for ther was
an other king in scotlande that hanged John Armestrang with his
fellowes / **And Sym** the larde and many other moe / which had paci-
fied the countrey / and stanched thifte / but he had lefte one thing
vndon / whiche perteynde aswell to his charge as th[other] [Fol. 138*b*]
And whene he was asked what that was he made a long narracion /
of the oppression of the poor / by the taking of the corse presaunte
beistes / and of the herying of poor men / by concistorye lawe / and
of many other abussions of the sprituall[itie] and churche / withe
many long stories and auctorities [and] thene the **Busshope** roise
and rebuked hym / saying [it] effered not to hym to speake such
matiers / commaundinge hym scilence / or elles to suffer Dethe for
it / by thair lawe / **Therafter** roise the man of ~~lawe~~ armes / all[ed]ginge
the contrarie / and commaunded the poor man to speake / saying
thair abusion hade been over longe suffered / withoute any law[e].
Thene the poor man shewed the greate abusion of busshopes / Pre-
lettes / Abbottes / reving menes wifes and doughters / and holding thaym /
and of the maynteynyng of thair childer / and of thair over bying of
lordes and Barrons eldeste sones / to thair Doughters / where thoroughe
the nobilitie of the blode of the Realme was degenerate / and of the
greate superfluous rentes that perteyned to the churche / by reason
of over muche temporall landes given to thaym / whiche thaye proved
that the kinge might take boothe by the canon lawe / and civile lawe /
and of the greate abomynable vices that reiagne in clostures / and of
the common Bordelles / that was keped in closturs of nunnes / All
this prouit by Experience, and alsoe was shewed **Thoffice** of a

~ *Appendix* ~

Busshope / and producit the newe testament *with* the auctorities to that effecte / and thene roise the Man of Armes / and the Burges / and did saye that all that was producit / by the poor **Man** and **Experence** / was reasonable / of veritie and of greate effecte / and verey expedient to be reafourmede / withe the consent of parliament / **And the Busshpe** said he would not consent therunto / **The Man of Armes and Burges** saide thay wer twoe / and he bot one / wherfor thair voice shuld haue mooste effecte / **Theraftre the King** in the playe / ratefied approved and confermed all that was rehersed.

NOTE

1. Sir William Eure's letter, Brit. Mus. MS. Reg. 7, C. xvi, fols. 137–39, is reprinted from Lindsay, *Works*, ed. Douglas Hamer, 2:2–6.

Bibliography

Allen, John W. *A History of Political Thought in the Sixteenth Century*. London: Methuen and Co. 1928.

Atkins, J. W. H. *English Literary Criticism: The Medieval Phase*. Cambridge: At the University Press, 1934.

Bale, John. *King Johan*. Edited by J. H. P. Pafford. The Malone Society Reprints. Oxford: Oxford University Press, 1931.

―――. *King Johan*. Edited by Barry B. Adams. San Marino, Calif.: The Huntington Library, 1969,

The Bannatyne Manuscript. Edited by W. Tod Ritchie. Vol. 3. Scottish Text Society. Edinburgh: William Blackwood and Sons, 1928.

Barclay, William R. "The Role of Sir David Lyndsay in the Scottish Reformation." Ph.D. dissertation, University of Wisconsin, 1956. *Dissertation Abstracts* 16 (1956): 2147.

Baumer, Franklin Le Van. *The Early Tudor Theory of Kingship*. New Haven: Yale University Press, 1940.

Bennett, H. S. *Chaucer and the Fifteenth Century*. Vol. 2, pt. 1 in *Oxford History of English Literature*. Oxford: Oxford University Press, 1954.

Bevington, David M. *From Mankind to Marlowe: Growth of Structure in the Popular Drama of Tudor England*. Cambridge, Mass.: Harvard University Press, 1962.

―――. *Tudor Drama and Politics*. Cambridge, Mass.: Harvard University Press, 1968.

Blatt, Thora Balslev. *The Plays of John Bale*. Copenhagen: G. E. C. Gad, 1968.

Bloomfield, Morton W. "Allegory as Interpretation." *New Literary History* 2 (1973): 301–17.

Brown, P. Hume. *John Knox*. 2 vols. London: Adam and Charles Black, 1895.

―――. *History of Scotland*. 2 vols. Cambridge: At the University Press, 1900–1902.

~ *Bibliography* ~

Buchanan, George. *Rerum Scoticarum Historia*. Translated by J. Aikman. 6 vols. Glasgow: Blackie and Son, 1856.

Burleigh, J. H. S. *A Church History of Scotland*. Oxford: Oxford University Press, 1960.

Calderwood, David. *History of the Kirk of Scotland*. Vol. 1, edited by Thomas Thomson. Edinburgh: The Woodrow Society, 1842.

Campbell, Lily Bess. *Divine Poetry and Drama in Sixteenth-Century England*. Berkeley: University of California Press, 1959.

Carlyle, R. W., and Carlyle, J. A. *Political Theory from 1300 to 1600*. Vol. 6 in *A History of Medieval Political Theory in the West*. Edinburgh: William Blackwood and Sons, 1936.

The Catechism of John Hamilton. Edited by Thomas Graves Law. Oxford: The Clarendon Press, 1884.

Chambers, E. K. *The Mediaeval Stage*. 2 vols. Oxford: Clarendon Press, 1903.

————. *The Elizabethan Stage*. 4 vols. Oxford: Clarendon Press, 1923.

Clemen, Wolfgang. *English Tragedy before Shakespeare*. Translated by T. S. Dorsch. London: Methuen & Co., 1961. (Originally published in German, 1955.)

The Complaynt of Scotlande. Edited by James A. H. Murray. Early English Text Society, ex. ser. 17 London: N. Trübner and Co., 1872–73.

The Court of Sapience. Edited by Robert Spindler. *Beitrage zur Englischen Philologie*, no. 6. Leipzig: Verlag von Bernhard Tauchnitz, 1927.

Craig, Hardin. *English Religious Drama*. Oxford: The Clarendon Press, 1955.

Craik, T. W. *The Tudor Interlude*. Leicester, England: Leicester University Press, 1958.

Critical Approaches to Medieval Literature. Selected Papers from the English Institute, 1958–1959. Edited by Dorothy Bethurum. New York: Columbia University Press, 1960.

Davies, W. T. "A Bibliography of John Bale," *Proceedings and Papers of the Oxford Bibliographical Society* 5 (1936–37): 201–79.

Davis, Norman. *Non-Cycle Plays and Fragments*. Early English Text Society. London: Oxford University Press, 1970.

Dickinson, William Croft. *Scotland from the Earliest Times to 1603*. Vol. 2 in *A New History of Scotland*. London: Thomas Nelson & Sons, 1961.

A Diurnal of Remarkable Occurents . . . in Scotland Since the Date of King James the Fourth till the Year 1575. Edited by Thomas Thomson. Edinburgh: The Bannatyne Club, 1833.

Donaldson, Gordon. *The Scottish Reformation*. Cambridge: At the University Press, 1960.

————. *Scotland: James V–James VII*. Vol. III in *The Edinburgh History of Scotland*. Edinburgh: Oliver & Boyd, 1965.

Douglas, Gawin. *The Shorter Poems*. Edited by Priscilla J. Bawcutt. Edinburgh, Scottish Text Society 1967.

Dunbar, William. *The Poems of* ————. Edited by W. Mackay Mackenzie. London: Faber and Faber, 1932.

Dunning, T. P. *Piers Plowman: An Interpretation of the A-Text*. Dublin: Talbot Press, 1937.

Durkan, John. "The Cultural Background in Sixteenth-Century Scotland." In *Essays on the Scottish Reformation*, edited by David McRoberts. Glasgow: Burns, 1962.

Elyot, Sir Thomas. *The Governor*. Edited by H. H. S. Croft. 2 vols. London: C. Kegan Paul, 1880.

Erasmus, Desiderius. *Education of a Christian Prince*. Translated by Lester K. Born. Columbia Records of Civilization Series. New York: Columbia University Press, 1936.

Farnham, Willard. *The Medieval Heritage of Elizabethan Tragedy*. Berkeley: University of California Press, 1936.

Ferguson, Arthur B. *The Articulate Citizen and the English Renaissance*. Durham, N.C.: Duke University Press, 1965.

Fisher, John Hurt. *John Gower*. New York: New York University Press, 1964.

Fletcher, Angus. *Allegory, the Theory of a Symbolic Mode*. Ithaca: Cornell University Press, 1964.

The Floure and the Leafe and The Assembly of Ladies. Edited D. A. Pearsall. London: Thomas Nelson and Sons, 1962.

Frank, R. W., Jr. "The Art of Reading Medieval Personification Allegory." *ELH* 20 (1953): 237–50.

Foxe, John. *Acts and Monuments*. Edited by George Townsend. Vols. 4 and 5. London: Seeley, Burnside and Seeley, 1846.

Gierke, Otto von. *Political Theories of the Middle Ages*. Translated by Frederic W. Maitland. Cambridge: At the University Press, 1913.

Gilbert of the Haye's Prose Manuscript. Edited by J. H. Stevenson. Vol. 2. Scottish Text Society. Edinburgh: William Blackwood and Sons, 1914.

Gower, John. *The Complete Works of John Gower*. Edited by George C. Macauley. Vol. 4. Oxford: The Clarendon Press, 1902.

———. *The Major Latin Work of John Gower*. Translated by Eric W. Stockton. Seattle: University of Washington Press, 1962.

———. *Selections*. Edited by J. A. W. Bennett. Oxford: The Clarendon Press, 1968.

Habicht, Werner. *Studien zur Dramenform vor Shakespeare*. Heidelberg: Anglistische Forschungen, 1969.

The Hamilton Papers. Edited by Joseph Bain. 2 vols. Edinburgh: H. M. General Register House, 1890.

Hamilton's Catechism and the Two-Penny Faith. Preface by Alexander F. Mitchell. Edinburgh: William Blackwood and Sons, 1882.

Harbage, Alfred. *Annals of English Drama*. Revised by S. Schoenbaum. London: Methuen, 1964.

Harris, William O. *Skelton's Magnyfycence and the Cardinal Virtue Tradition*. Chapel Hill: University of North Carolina Press, 1965.

Hawes, Stephen. *The Example of Virtue*. London: W. de Worde, 1510. STC no. 12945.

Heiserman, Arthur R. *Skelton and Satire*. Chicago: University of Chicago Press, 1962.

Herkless, John. *Cardinal Beaton*. Edinburgh: William Blackwood and Sons, 1891.

Herkless, John, and Hannay, Robert K. *The Archbishops of Saint Andrews*. Vol. 4. Edinburgh: William Blackwood and Sons, 1915.

Herrick, Marvin T. *Comic Theory in the Sixteenth Century*. Urbana: University of Illinois Press, 1950. Reissued in paperback, 1964.

Hoccleve, Thomas. *The Regement of Princes*. Edited by F. J. Furnivall. Early English Text Society, ex. ser. 72. London: Kegan Paul, Trench, Trubner and Co., 1897.

Houk, R. A. "Versions of Lindsay's *Satire of the Three Estates*." *PMLA* 55 (1940): 396–405.

Houle, Peter J. *The English Morality and Related Drama, A Bibliographical Survey*. Hamden, Conn.: The Shoe String Press, 1972.

Howell, Wilbur Samuel. *Logic and Rhetoric in England, 1500–1700*. Princeton: Princeton University Press, 1956.

Jackson, W. T. H. "Allegory and Allegorization." *Research Studies* (Washington State University) 32 (1964): 161–75.

Jauss, Hans-Robert. "Litterature médiévale et théorie des genres." *Poetique*; *Revue de Theorie et d'analyses Litteraires* 1 (1970): 79–101.

———. "Literary History as a Challenge to Literary Theory." *New Literary History* 1 (1970): 7–37.

Kelly, Douglas. "The Scope of the Treatment of Composition in the Twelfth and Thirteenth-Century Arts of Poetry." *Speculum* 41 (1966): 261–78.

Knox, John. *The Works of John Knox*. Edited by David Laing. 6 vols. Edinburgh: The Bannatyne Club, 1846–64.

———. *History of the Reformation in Scotland*. A modernized edition by William Croft Dickinson. 2 vols. London: Thomas Nelson and Sons, 1949.

Lauder, William. *Extant Works*. Edited by Fitzedward Hall and F. J. Furnivall. Early English Text Society, orig. ser. 3, 41. London: N. Trübner and Co., 1870.

Lee, Maurice, Jr. "John Knox and His History." *Scottish Historical Review* 14 (1966): 79–88.

Lesley, John. *History of Scotland*. Edited by Thomas Thomson. Edinburgh: The Bannatyne Club, 1830.

Letters of James V. Edited by Denys Hay. Edinburgh: Her Majesty's Stationery Office, 1954.

Lewis, C. S. *The Allegory of Love*. Oxford: Oxford University Press, 1936. Reprinted with corrections, 1938; reprinted in paperback, 1958.

Lindesay of Pitscottie, Robert. *The Historie and Chronicles of Scotland*. Edited by Aeneas J. G. MacKay. 2 vols. Scottish Text Society. Edinburgh: William Blackwood and Sons, 1899.

~ *Bibliography* ~

Lindsay, Sir David. *The Tragical Death of David Beaton*. Preface by Roberte Burrant. London: Day and Seres, [1548?]. STC no. 15683.

———. *Works of Sir David Lindsay*. Edited by Douglas Hamer. 4 vols. Scottish Text Society. Edinburgh: William Blackwood and Sons, 1931–36.

———. *The Satire of the Three Estates*. Edinburgh Festival Version by Robert Kemp. London: William Heineman, 1951.

———. *Ane Satyre of the Thrie Estaitis*. Edited by James Kinsley. London: Cassell, 1954.

———. *A Satire of the Three Estates*. Adapted by Matthew McDiarmid from the acting text by Robert Kemp. London: Heinemann Educational Books, 1967.

Lydgate, John. *Secress of Old Philisoffres. A version of the "Secreta Secretorum."* Edited by Robert Steele. Early English Text Society, ex. ser. 66. London: Kegan Paul, Trench, Trubner and Co., 1894.

———. *Fall of Princes*. Edited by Henry Bergen. 4 vols. Early English Text Society, ex. ser. 191–94. London: Kegan Paul, Trench, Trubner and Co., 1918–19.

———. *The Pilgrimage of the Life of Man*. Edited by F. J. Furnivall. 3 vols. Early English Text Society, ex. ser. 77, 83, 92. London: Kegan Paul, Trench, Trubner and Co., 1899–1904.

M'Crie, Thomas. *Life of Andrew Melville*. 2 vols. 2d ed. Edinburgh: William Blackwood and Sons, 1824.

Macewen, A. R. *A History of the Church in Scotland*. 2 vols. London: Hodder and Stoughton, 1913, 1918.

Mackenzie, William Roy. *The English Moralities from the Point of View of Allegory*. Harvard Studies in English, 2 Boston: Ginn and Co., 1914.

McKeon, Richard. "Rhetoric in the Middle Ages." *Speculum* 17 (1942): 1–32.

MacQueen, John. "Ane Satyre of the Thrie Estaitis." *Studies in Scottish Literature* 3 (1966): 129–43.

———. *Robert Henryson*. Oxford: The Clarendon Press, 1967.

———, ed. *Ballatis of Luve*. Edinburgh: Edinburgh University Press, 1970.

———. *Allegory*. London: Methuen, 1970.

The Maitland Folio Manuscript. Edited by W. A. Craigie. Vol. 1. Scottish Text Society. Edinburgh: William Blackwood and Sons, 1919.

Mayer, C. A. " 'Satyre' as a Dramatic Genre." *Bibliotheque d'Humanisme et Renaissance* 13 (1951): 327–33.

Mill, Anna Jean. *Mediaeval Plays in Scotland*. Saint Andrews University Publications, no. 24. Edinburgh: William Blackwood and Sons, 1927.

———. "The Influence of the Continental Drama on Lyndsay's 'Satyre of the Thrie Estaitis.' " *Modern Language Review* 25 (1930): 425–42.

———. "Representations of Lyndsay's *Satyre of the Thrie Estaitis*." *PMLA* 47 (1932): 636–49. Addendum in *PNLA* 48 (1933): 315–16.

———. "The Original Version of Lindsay's *Satyre of the Thrie Estaitis*." *Studies in Scottish Literature* 6 (1968), 67–75.

Miller, Edwin S. "The Christening of the Three Estates." *MLN* 60 (1945): 42–44.

Mitchell, Jerome. *Thomas Hoccleve*. Urbana: University of Illinois Press, 1968.

Mohl, Ruth. *The Three Estates in Medieval and Renaissance Literature*. New York: Columbia University Press, 1933.

Montgomery, Robert L., Jr. "Allegory and the Incredible Fable: The Italian View from Dante to Tasso." *PMLA* 81 (1966): 45–55.

Mozley, J. F. *John Foxe and His Book*. London: Society for Promoting Christian Knowledge, 1940.

Mum and the Soothsayer. Edited by Mabel Day and Robert Steele. Early English Text Society, 199. London: Kegan Paul, Trench, Trubner and Co., 1936.

Murison, W. *Sir David Lyndsay*. Cambridge: At the University Press, 1938.

Newman, F. X., ed. *The Meaning of Courtly Love*. Albany: State University of New York Press, 1969.

Piers Plowman. Edited by W. W. Skeat. 2 vols. Oxford: Oxford University Press, 1886.

Pollet, Maurice. *John Skelton*. Translated by John Warrington. London: Dent, 1971.

Renoir, Alain. *The Poetry of John Lydgate*. London: Routledge and Kegan Paul, 1967.

Reson and Sensuallyte. Edited by Ernst Sieper. 2 vols. Early English Text Society, ex. ser. 84, 89. London: Kegan Paul, Trench, Trubner and Co., 1903.

Respublica. Edited by W. W. Gregg. Early English Text Society, o.s. 226. London: Kegan Paul, Trench, Trubner and Co., 1952.

Rey-Flaud, Henri. *Le Cercle Magique*. Paris: Gallimard, 1973.

Ridley, Jasper. *John Knox*. Oxford: Oxford University Press, 1968.

Rolland, John. *The Court of Venus*. Edited by Walter Gregor. Scottish Text Society. Edinburgh: William Blackwood and Sons, 1883–84.

Rossiter, A. P. *English Drama from the Earliest Times to Elizabeth*. London: Hutchinson and Co., 1950.

Ryan, Lawrence V. "Doctrine and Dramatic Structure in *Everyman*." *Speculum* 32 (1957): 722–35.

Sadler, Sir Ralph. *The State Papers and Letters of Sir Ralph Sadler*. Edited by Arthur Clifford. 2 vols. Edinburgh: Archibald Constable and Co., 1809.

Schirmer, Walter F. *John Lydgate*. Translated by Ann E. Keep. Berkeley: University of California Press, 1961. Originally published in German: Tubingen, 1952.

Skelton, John. *Magnyfycence*. Edited by Robert Lee Ramsay. Early English Text Society, ex. ser. 98. London: Kegan Paul, Trench, Trubner and Co., 1906 (issued in 1908).

Smith, Lacey Baldwin. "The 'Taste for Tudors' Since 1940." In *Changing Views on British History: Essays on Historical Writing since 1939*, edited by Elizabeth C. Furber. Cambridge, Mass.: Harvard University Press, 1966. Originally published in *Studies in the Renaissance* 7 (1960): 167–83.

~ Bibliography ~

Southern, Richard. *The Medieval Theatre in the Round: A Study of the Staging of the "Castle of Perseverance" and Related Matters*. London: Faber and Faber, 1957.

————. *The Staging of Plays Before Shakespeare*. London: Faber and Faber, 1973.

Spivack, Bernard. *Shakespeare and the Allegory of Evil*. New York: Columbia University Press, 1958.

Spottiswoode, John. *History of the Church of Scotland*. Edited by M. Russell and Mark Napier. 3 vols. Edinburgh: Bannatyne Club and Spottiswoode Society, 1847–51.

Statua Ecclesiae Scoticanae. Edited by Joseph Robertson. Vol. 2. Edinburgh: Archibald Constable, 1866.

Statutes of the Scottish Church, 1225–1559. Translated by David Patrick. Scottish History Society, no. 54. Edinburgh: Edinburgh University Press, 1907.

Stratman, Carl. *Bibliography of Medieval Drama*. 2d ed. New York: Frederick Ungar, 1972.

Sweeting, Elizabeth J. *Early Tudor Criticism*. Oxford: Basil Blackwell, 1940.

Teulet, Alexandre, ed. *Relations Politiques de la France et de L'Espagne avec L'Écosse au XVIᵉ siècle*. 5 vols. Paris: Libraire de la Société de l'histoire de France, 1862.

Thompson, E. N. S. "The English Moral Play." *Transactions of the Connecticut Academy of Arts and Sciences* 14 (1908–10): 291–415.

Traver, Hope. *The Four Daughters of God. A Study of the Versions of This Allegory with Especial Reference to Those in Latin, French, and English*. Bryn Mawr College Monographs, Bryn Mawr, Pa., 1907.

————. "The Four Daughters of God: A Mirror of Changing Doctrine." *PMLA* 40 (1925): 44–92.

Tuve, Rosemund. *Allegorical Imagery: Some Mediaeval Books and their Posterity*. Princeton: Princeton University Press, 1966.

Two Missions of Jacques de la Brosse. Edited by Gladys Dickinson. Scottish History Society, ser. 3, vol. 36. Edinburgh: Edinburgh University Press, 1942.

Utley, Francis Lee. *The Crooked Rib, an Analytic Index to the Argument about Women in English and Scots Literature to the End of the Year, 1568*. Columbus: Ohio State University Press, 1944.

Waith, Eugene M. "*Controversia* in the English Drama: Medwall and Massinger." *PMLA* 68 (1953): 286–303.

Wickham, Glynne. *Early English Stages 1300–1660*. Vols. 1 and 2, pt. 1. London: Routledge and Kegan Paul, 1959–63.

Wilson, F. P. *The English Drama 1485–1585*. Vol. 4, pt. 1 in *Oxford History of English Literature*. Oxford: The Clarendon Press, 1969.

Wimsatt, James I. *Allegory and Mirror: Tradition and Structure in Middle English Literature*. New York: Pegasus Press, 1971.

Acknowledgments

Although this book must stand or fall on its own merits or failings, the author owes much to many people. Above all, I am grateful to Professor Theodore Silverstein of the University of Chicago. He first introduced me to the pleasures of medieval literature as a graduate student and continues to provide that unfailing patience and sympathy which encourages his students to find their own voices. To me, he is a model of gentilesse in its true meaning.

It seems only courteous, too, to thank the scholars who have written on allegory and on the morality play, in general. If I seem to disagree with many, it is disagreement in the spirit of a debating society which argues for love of the process and the point. Surely, no one can participate in that society without learning how much one depends on the work of others. In this context, I should especially mention the books of C. S. Lewis and Willard Farnham, books that first taught me about the subject and that I respect no less because I have come to disagree with them. Less immediate, perhaps, is my gratitude for the work of Elder Olson and of H. D. F. Kitto. Although neither of these writers on drama are concerned with the morality play, I have learned much about basic critical method from their books.

And then there are the many debts acquired when a manuscript is written around and between periods of intense living. For a book so short, this has been long nurtured with the thinking of several years. At a very early stage, Professor Jerome Taylor of the University of Wisconsin and Professor David Bevington of Chicago kindly let me profit from their reading of the first draft. My former colleagues at

~ *Acknowledgments* ~

Marymount College, Tarrytown, New York, provided an intellectual environment filled with a warmth and good humor which I shall always remember with gratitude. At Kent State University, I have enjoyed the facilities and company which enabled me to put the manuscript into final form. Jane Benson of Interlibrary Loan and the library staff provided books and answered my many questions. I have used with pleasure, too, the facilities of the libraries at the University of Chicago, at Columbia University, and, during 1969–70, those at Oxford University.

My more immediate debts of publication belong to *Comparative Drama* and to *Studies in Scottish Literature* for permission to reprint portions of this book which first appeared in their pages in different form. I should thank, too, the American Council of Learned Societies for a grant-in-aid during 1971–72; although not directly connected with this book, my work during that period has provided some useful background which, inevitably, is interwoven here. The Research Council of Kent State University provided funds for typing costs.

Finally, one comes to the most personal debts. My two small sons, Alexander and Edward, graced my days with some periods of quiet. My husband, Nathan Kantrowitz, combining his own sociology with an active interest in my literature, first taught me the interest of politics. Although he neither types nor proofreads, his delight in the intellect has helped my own work as only an exemplary husband can.

My thanks go to all those who helped with this book. I am solely responsible for any errors it may contain.

J. S. K.

Index